THE GR

MW00364920

Trekking the
HADRIAN'S
WALL PATH

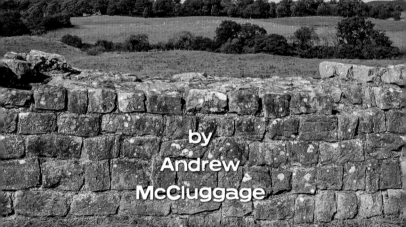

by
Andrew
McCluggage

KNIFE
EDGE
Outdoor Guidebooks

About the Author

Andrew McCluggage is an outdoor writer and photographer from Northern Ireland. After 20 years as a corporate lawyer, he decided to do something interesting and started writing walking guidebooks.

His first book was Walking in the Briançonnais, covering a beautiful part of the French Alps. Since then, he has written a variety of guidebooks for hiking and trekking.

Other Knife Edge Outdoor Guidebooks written by Andrew include:

► The Mourne Mountains

► Northern Ireland: The Unmissable Walks

► Tour du Mont Blanc

► Trekking the Dolomites AV1

► Walker's Haute Route: Chamonix to Zermatt

► Trekking the Corsica GR20

► Walking Chamonix-Mont Blanc

► Walking Brittany

► Tour of the Écrins National Park (GR54)

Sycamore Gap (Stage 3e)

Scale for OS map extracts

0   ©Crown Copyright 2020   1km

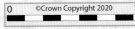

Publisher: Knife Edge Outdoor Limited (NI648568)
12 Torrent Business Centre, Donaghmore, County Tyrone, BT70 3BF, UK
www.knifeedgeoutdoor.com

First edition 2021

A catalogue record for this book is available from the British Library.

Front cover: Sewingshields Crags (Stage 3d)
Title page: Hadrian's Wall just east of Birdoswald Fort (Stage 4d)
This page: The section of Hadrian's Wall at Black Carts (Stage 3b)

All routes described in this guide have been recently walked by the author and
both the author and publisher have made all reasonable efforts to ensure that
all information is as accurate as possible. However, while a printed book remains
constant for the life of an edition, things in the countryside often change. Trails are
subject to forces outside our control: for example, landslides, tree-falls or other
matters can result in damage to paths or route changes; waymarks and signposts
may fade or be destroyed by wind, snow or the passage of time; or trails may not
be maintained by the relevant authorities. If you notice any discrepancies between
the contents of this guide and the facts on the ground, then please let us know.
Our contact details can be found at the back of this book.

Contents

Getting Help

Emergency services number: dial 999

Distress signal

The signal that you are in distress is 6 blasts on a whistle spaced over a minute, followed by a minute's silence. Then repeat. The acknowledgment that your signal has been received is 3 blasts of a whistle over a minute followed by a minute's silence. At night, flashes of a torch can also be used in the same sequences. **Always carry a torch and whistle.**

Signalling to a helicopter from the ground

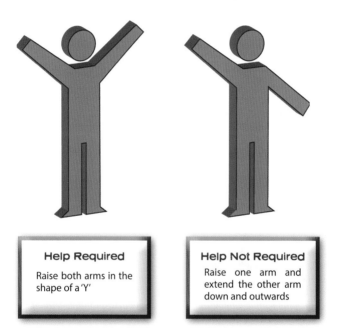

Help Required	Help Not Required
Raise both arms in the shape of a 'Y'	Raise one arm and extend the other arm down and outwards

WARNING

Hills, cliffs and mountains can be dangerous places and walking is a potentially dangerous activity. Many of the routes described in this guide cross exposed and potentially hazardous terrain. You walk entirely at your own risk. It is solely your responsibility to ensure that you and all members of your group have adequate experience, fitness and equipment. Neither the author nor the publisher accepts any responsibility or liability whatsoever for death, injury, loss, damage or inconvenience resulting from use of this book, participation in the activity of mountain walking or otherwise.

Some land may be privately owned so we cannot guarantee that there is a legal right of entry to the land. Occasionally, routes change as a result of land disputes.

The path on top of HW at Housesteads Fort (Stage 3e)

Introduction

The Romans were famous for their engineering prowess and Hadrian's Wall ('HW') was one of their finest works. When completed, it ran for 73 miles between the west and east coasts of what is now Northern England. The Wall, which is an UNESCO World Heritage Site, passed with barely a break across the crags and hills of some of Britain's wildest terrain. And yet the Romans managed to complete it in less than a decade. Despite the ravages of the intervening centuries, many sections of the Wall are still standing today and you can view most of them on the Hadrian's Wall Path ('HWP').

Of all the world's long-distance treks, the HWP is utterly unique and it is one of England's official 'National Trails'. It follows the line of HW, all the way across England, between Bowness-on-Solway on the W coast and Wallsend in the E. Along the route, the trekker passes countless Roman ruins including fabulously preserved forts and, of course, long stretches of the Wall itself. Surely, no other long-distance route can claim to display so much of historical interest. In fact, there is so much Roman history to absorb that you find yourself fully immersed in it, constantly imagining life as a soldier on the Wall. It is a fascinating and unforgettable experience.

The scenery is magnificent too. Away from the cities of Carlisle and Newcastle, you will hike some of England's most remote terrain and some of its loveliest farmland too. The central section of the trek leads you across the Pennines and through the wild and beautiful Northumberland National Park ('NNP') which is so remote that the absence of light pollution makes it one of the darkest places at night in the UK: campers often enjoy spectacular night skies.

Notwithstanding statistics published elsewhere, we find that the HWP route is 87 miles (139km) in length with approximately 6700ft (2000m) of ascent. If those statistics sound intimidating then do not worry: with the right preparation, planning and approach, the HWP is perfectly manageable for most people of reasonable fitness. Yes it is a challenge but it is an achievable one. And that is where this book comes in! Most of what you need to know to plan, and prepare for, the HWP is here within these pages. And the entire route is described in detail to guide you on the trek itself. Furthermore, unlike some other books, this one contains real Ordnance Survey maps: for each stage, there are 1:25,000 scale maps to go with the accurate and concise route descriptions. Because all the maps are set out within the guidebook itself, there is no need to fumble about with a guidebook in one hand and a map in the other.

Castle Nick (Milecastle 39): Stage 3e

Ask the Author

If you have any questions which are not answered by this book, then you can ask the author on our Facebook group, **'Hadrian's Wall Path Q&A'**. The group's URL is **www.facebook.com/ groups/HadriansWall**

We aim to ensure that you have the best chance possible of completing the trek. We place great importance on the correct preparation and we focus in detail on modern lightweight equipment (see 'Equipment'). We also believe that it is crucial to match your itinerary to your experience, fitness and ability. Accordingly, we have included here an extraordinary level of detail on itinerary planning: our unique itinerary planner has 14 different itineraries to choose from. For each itinerary, we have completed for you all the difficult calculations of time, distance and altitude gain/loss. This makes it easy for you to design a manageable itinerary that suits your specific needs. Once on the trail, you will be able to relax and fully enjoy one of the world's great treks.

How hard is the HWP?

Notwithstanding the challenges, many thousands of hikers walk the full length of the HWP each year. It is therefore an achievable endeavour. However, you will need to walk a significant distance each day so a reasonable level of fitness is required. That said, the HWP has much less climbing and descending than many other treks and it is considered to be one of the easiest multi-day hikes in the UK. In fact, there are only 6600ft (2000m) of ascent and descent on the entire trek and a large proportion of that is found in the central section (Stages 3a to 4d). This means that, whichever direction you hike the HWP, you will not reach the more hilly and challenging stages until after you have warmed-up on the flatter sections.

For the most part, the HWP uses clear paths and tracks which are simple to negotiate. There are also some short sections along minor roads. The route is well marked. Most people walk the HWP in five to eight days. However, very fit and experienced hikers can do it in four days and runners often do it even faster. Others prefer to walk more slowly and take nine or ten days, soaking up all of the historic delights on offer, visiting every fort and museum and enjoying the real ale in the country pubs along the way. There is plenty of accommodation scattered across the trail so the HWP can be as hard or easy as you like.

Direction and start/finish points

The HWP runs between Wallsend in the E and Bowness-on-Solway in the W. You can hike it in either direction so this book describes both approaches in full.

Academics have determined that HW was largely built E-W so the milecastles and turrets have been numbered in that direction. The logic of passing these structures in ascending order may explain why the convention is to walk E-W. However, there are more sensible reasons for hiking W. Firstly, Bowness-on-Solway is a nicer place to finish than Wallsend: travelling through the inner city of Newcastle is undoubtedly an anti-climatic way to finish an otherwise beautiful trek. Secondly, in our opinion, some key highlights of the trek are better viewed looking W so it makes sense to walk in that direction: of course it is entirely subjective, but we think that Sewingshields Crags (Stage 3d), for example, is epic when viewed facing W. Thirdly, as the majority of people walk E-W, this is probably the more sociable approach: you are more likely to bump into the same people each day making it easier to develop trail friendships.

However, there are also good reasons for tackling the trek W-E. The most significant factor is wind direction: the prevailing winds in the UK are from the SW or W. So if you walk W-E, there is a higher probability that the wind will be on your back: you expend less energy walking away from the wind. However, there are no guarantees when it comes to the elements: during the research for this book, we hiked the HWP in both directions and we walked into the wind on both occasions!

It can also be argued that Newcastle is a more convenient place to finish: there are numerous travel options so it is easier to get away from there than from Bowness-on-Solway. Furthermore, the numerous bars and restaurants in Newcastle allow for an exuberant celebration upon completion of the trek: Bowness-on-Solway, on the other hand, only has one pub.

In this book, we cater for both E-W and W-E trekkers: route descriptions and a variety of itineraries are given for each approach. The numbered waypoints on the real maps make the route descriptions simple to follow in either direction.

Hiking shorter sections of the HWP

Walking the HWP in one go is a wonderful experience but there are other ways to enjoy this incredible trail. If you do not wish to walk the entire route, it is possible to walk shorter sections of it. There are numerous escape/access points along the route where you could leave or join the trek using public transport or taxis: see 'Secondary trail-heads'. You could start at any of these places and walk a few sections. Or you could skip sections by leaving the route at one of these points.

Furthermore, a great many people prefer to hike the HWP in day-long sections using public transport to travel to/from the start and finish points: see 'Public Transport along Hadrian's Wall'. Over the course of months or years, they will eventually complete the entire trek. Many others have no desire to walk the HWP in its entirety and simply want to experience a few of its highlights. The Itinerary Planner should help you to plan day-walks along the HWP. Often day-walkers hike in groups, leaving a car at each end of their route.

Guided tours, self-guided tours or independent walking?

A frequently asked question is whether to walk independently or with an organised group. The answer is a personal one, depending upon your own particular circumstances and requirements. For many, the decision to organise the trek themselves, and to walk independently, can be almost life-changing, opening the door for other challenges in the future. There is much satisfaction to be gained in planning and navigating a trek yourself and the sense of achievement on completion is to be savoured.

However, the independent trekker usually carries a full pack and is responsible for all daily decisions such as pacing; which way to go at junctions; when to stock up with food and water; and choice of route in bad weather. For some, this will be too great a burden on top of the physical effort required simply to walk the route. For those walkers, a guided group is a great solution: the tour company typically organises food, accommodation and (if possible) transfer of luggage each night. And the guide makes all the decisions, enabling the walker to concentrate on the walking. There are a few tour companies operating guided trips on the HWP but most do not cover the full official route. Often the tours focus only on the highlights of HW. Many are centre-based meaning that you return to the same hotel each night.

Self-guided tours are much more popular and are a sensible middle-ground. The tour company books all the accommodation and provides all the advice and information required to complete the trek. However, you will walk the trail without a guide. Normally, your breakfast will be provided and you can request packed lunches. For evening meals, they will provide details of pubs and restaurants which are walking distance from your accommodation. Often they can transfer your baggage to your accommodation each night so you only need to carry a small day-pack on the trail.

There are also many businesses offering accommodation booking services only: they do not offer advice on the trek itself. In fact, these days there are so many self-guided tour companies and accommodation booking services that much of the accommodation along the HWP is block-booked months in advance. At peak times, this makes it harder for the independent trekker to secure first choice accommodation unless booked well in advance. As a result, many confident trekkers (who would be perfectly capable of walking independently) book a self-guided trip simply to avail of the accommodation booking service. By booking a self-guided tour or using an accommodation booking service, much of the stress and hassle of planning the trek are alleviated, albeit at a price.

St. Michael's Church, Burgh-by-Sands (Stage 6b)

When to go

In theory you could tackle the HWP at almost any time of year (weather permitting). Even in winter, there is rarely snow in sufficient quantities to prevent normal hiking. However, the main trekking season runs from Easter to October. Often the weather permits trekking outside those months but it is discouraged by the authorities responsible for maintaining the trail because the ground is wetter and more prone to erosion. Unlike on other trails, erosion does not simply damage the local environment: it also puts the underlying Roman ruins at risk, many of which have never been excavated. It is for this reason, the HWP Passport Scheme (see page 48) only operates between Easter and 31 October. Before Easter and after October, some accommodation will be closed.

Spring (March to May): this can be the most beautiful time of year for walking. Many wild-flowers are on show and the gorse will also be in full bloom with its vivid yellow flowers and coconut aroma. By May, new growth will be upon the deciduous plants and grass is at its greenest. The weather is often sunny and warm. Indeed, May can be the finest month in England and in recent years, the weather in May has tended to be more favourable than in July and August. Visibility in spring is generally excellent so views are wide-ranging. Of course, rain is still a possibility at this time of year but it usually decreases as the season progresses. Early in spring, the number of walkers is low (except at Easter), gradually increasing throughout the season.

Summer (June to August): this is the peak walking season and visitor numbers are at their greatest. The days are long and statistically, your chances of good weather are highest in this period. Often June is the best month and August is sometimes unsettled. Temperatures are at their peak and there is sometimes haze. Summer also sees the heather in full bloom, covering hillsides with a beautiful purple carpet.

Season	Pros	Cons
Spring	Pleasant temperatures Frequent sunny skies Good visibility Gorse and wild-flowers Fewer visitors	Rainy spells are common in March and April Ground can be wet
Summer	Generally reliably fine weather Heather season	Sometimes hazy Visitor numbers highest
Autumn	Pleasant temperatures Frequent sunny skies Excellent visibility Fewer visitors Autumn colours	Shorter days Cooler evenings
Winter	Sometimes crisp clear skies Excellent visibility Fewer visitors	Shortest days Can be cold and icy Occasionally, there is snow

Autumn (September to November): September is still a busy month on the HWP but visitor numbers reduce, and some accommodation closes, as the season progresses. Autumn sometimes provides the best walking conditions: the weather in September and October can be more settled, with less rain, than in summer. Temperatures are lower but still comfortable. Skies can be very clear giving excellent visibility and the quality of the low light is magnificent. The wide variety of deciduous plants in the UK means that the autumn colours are stunning. However, as the days get shorter, it is wise to start walking early. If something were to go wrong, you would have less daylight in which to seek help than in summer.

Winter (December to February): these are the coldest months and, although snow can lie on the hills, heavy falls are not that common these days. A light sprinkling of snow can be a delight for a suitably-equipped walker although care should be taken. However, walking in deep snow is best left to those with the appropriate winter mountain experience and the correct equipment. Even if there is no snow, watch out for ice which forms in the many places where water collects. Cold months often bring crisp, clear weather and the low sun makes the light very beautiful. A sunny day in winter can be one of the best of the year. Days are short so start early

Boustead Hill (Stage 6b/6c)

Using this book

This book is designed to be used by walkers of differing abilities. Many guidebooks for long-distance treks rigidly divide the route into a fixed number of long day stages, leaving it up to the walker to break down those stages to design daily routes which suit his/her abilities. This book, however, has been laid out differently to give the trekker flexibility: it divides the route into 28 shorter stages which can be combined to design daily routes to meet your own specific needs.

Each of the 28 stages covers the distance between one accommodation option and the subsequent one. Almost every accommodation option on the entire route is the start/finish point of a stage. You can choose how many of these stages you wish to walk each day. Each stage has its own walk description, route map, elevation profile and beautiful photos.

The labelling of the stages uses a combination of numbers and letters. It is a simple system but requires a little bit of explanation. Firstly, we have divided the route into six 'Sections' (numbered from 1 to 6): each Section represents one day of our standard 6-day schedule. Within each Section, the route is broken down into stages: every stage is labelled with a number between 1 and 6 representing the relevant Section that the stage is part of. Every stage is also labelled (in order from E-W) with a letter. So, for example, the first stage in Section 4 would be 'Stage 4a', the next stage would be 'Stage 4b' and so on. Take a look at the detailed Itinerary Planner below and all should become clear.

The Itinerary Planner includes a range of tables outlining 14 suggested itineraries of 3, 4, 5, 6, 7, 8 and 9 days. We include itineraries for both E-W and W-E walkers. In each table, the maths have been done for you so there is no need for you to waste time (and mental strength!) working out daily distances, timings and height gain.

Of course, the suggested itineraries are only suggestions. You can shorten or lengthen your day in any number of ways to suit yourself: just decide how many stages you want to walk that day. It is up to you. As there is accommodation at the end of each stage, it is easy to design your own bespoke itinerary and adjust it on the ground as you go along.

For example, day 1 of the standard 6-day route involves walking Stages 1a, 1b and 1c. But you could decide to extend your day 1 by walking Stages 1a, 1b, 1c and 2a, all on the same day. Or you might be tired and decide to shorten your day by walking only Stages 1a and 1b. With some other guidebooks, you would have to work out how to split stages yourself, involving some complicated maths to plan distances and times going forward. This guide, however, does all the hard mental work for you.

In this book:

Timings indicate the approximate time required by a reasonably fit walker to complete a stage. They do not include stoppage time. Do not get frustrated if your own times do not match ours: everyone walks at different speeds. As you progress through the trek, you will soon learn how your own times compare with those given here and you will adjust your plans accordingly.

Walking distances are given in both miles and kilometres (km). One mile equates to approximately 1.6km.

Place names in brackets in the route descriptions indicate the direction to be followed on signposts. For example, "('Newcastle')" would mean that you follow a sign for Newcastle.

Ascent/descent numbers are the aggregate of all the altitude gain or loss (measured in feet and metres) on the uphill or downhill sections of a stage. As a rule of thumb, a fit walker climbs 1000 to 1300 feet (300 to 400m) in an hour. The statistics tables in the route descriptions are based on E-W itineraries: W-E walkers should simply swap the ascent and descent figures.

Elevation profiles are provided for each Section, indicating where the climbs and descents fall on the route. The profile lines have been deliberately drawn in varying thickness purely for aesthetic purposes. Read the elevations off the top of the lines. The profiles are based on E-W itineraries: W-E walkers should simply read them in reverse.

Spellings of place names are normally derived from the OS maps. However, there is sometimes disagreement over how places are spelt. Accordingly, you may notice different spellings elsewhere.

Real maps are provided. These are extracts from 1:25,000 scale maps produced by Ordnance Survey, the mapping agency for GB. The maps are divided into 4cm grid squares: each square represents 1km x 1km. On the maps, we have marked the route of the trek, significant waypoints and the start/finish points of stages. Because there is accommodation near every start/finish point, we have not marked such accommodation specifically on the maps: however, accommodation located mid-stage is clearly marked. On each map, north is at the top of the page.

The following abbreviations are used:

BCE	Before the Common Era (a secular alternative to 'BC')
CE	The Common Era (a secular alternative to 'AD')
GB	Great Britain
HW/the 'Wall'	Hadrian's Wall
HWP	Hadrian's Wall Path
NNP	Northumberland National Park
OS	Ordnance Survey
TL	Turn left
TR	Turn right
SH	Straight ahead
N, S, E and W, etc.	North, South, East and West, etc.
E-W	East to west
W-E	West to east

The HWP heads along the cliffs above Crag Lough (Stage 3e)

Itinerary Planner

East to West

Stage	Start	Time (hr)	Distance		Ascent		Descent	
			miles	km	ft	m	ft	m
1a	Wallsend	2:00	5.1	8.2	72	22	98	30
1b	Newcastle Swing Bridge	2:45	6.7	10.7	184	56	148	45
1c	Newburn	1:30	3.6	5.8	427	130	66	20
2a	Heddon-on-the-Wall	1:00	2.4	3.9	180	55	213	65
2b	Ironsign	1:30	3.5	5.7	341	104	262	80
2c	Robin Hood Inn	1:30	3.3	5.3	302	92	164	50
2d	Halton Red House	2:30	5.6	9	492	150	558	170
2e	Wall exit	0:15	0.9	1.5	16	5	52	16
3a	Chollerford	1:30	2.7	4.3	571	174	98	30
3b	Green Carts Farm exit	1:15	2.4	3.8	279	85	180	55
3c	Carraw B&B	0:45	2.1	3.4	82	25	62	19
3d	Grindon exit	1:30	2.3	3.7	522	159	427	130
3e	Housesteads	1:45	3.2	5.2	686	209	673	205
4a	Steel Rigg (Once Brewed Exit)	1:15	2.5	4.1	328	100	673	205
4b	Cawfields Quarry	1:45	4.1	6.6	712	217	869	265
4c	Holmhead	0:45	1.9	3.1	131	40	197	60
4d	Gilsland	2:15	4.8	7.8	502	153	525	160
4e	Banks	0:30	1.1	1.7	121	37	279	85
5a	Lanercost exit	1:00	2.1	3.4	230	70	295	90
5b	Walton	0:45	2.0	3.2	125	38	148	45
5c	Newtown	1:00	2.4	3.9	0	0	164	50
5d	Bleatarn Farm	0:45	1.7	2.7	0	0	0	0
5e	Crosby Camping	2:00	5.1	8.2	0	0	0	0
6a	Carlisle (Sands Centre)	2:00	5.0	8.1	262	80	230	70
6b	Beaumont	1:30	3.9	6.3	82	25	180	55
6c	Boustead Hill	1:30	3.5	5.7	33	10	33	10
6d	Glasson	0:30	1.3	2.1	0	0	0	0
6e	Port Carlisle	0:30	1.3	2.1	33	10	0	0
Finish	Bowness-on-Solway							

Stage	Start	Time (hr)	Distance		Ascent		Descent	
			miles	km	ft	m	ft	m
6e	Bowness-on-Solway	0:30	1.3	2.1	0	0	33	10
6d	Port Carlisle	0:30	1.3	2.1	0	0	0	0
6c	Glasson	1:30	3.5	5.7	33	10	33	10
6b	Boustead Hill	1:30	3.9	6.3	180	55	82	25
6a	Beaumont	2:00	5.0	8.1	230	70	262	80
5e	Carlisle (Sands Centre)	2:00	5.1	8.2	0	0	0	0
5d	Crosby Camping	0:45	1.7	2.7	0	0	0	0
5c	Bleatarn Farm	1:00	2.4	3.9	164	50	0	0
5b	Newtown	0:45	2.0	3.2	148	45	125	38
5a	Walton	1:00	2.1	3.4	295	90	230	70
4e	Lanercost exit	0:30	1.1	1.7	279	85	121	37
4d	Banks	2:15	4.8	7.8	525	160	502	153
4c	Gilsland	0:45	1.9	3.1	197	60	131	40
4b	Holmhead	1:45	4.1	6.6	869	265	712	217
4a	Cawfields Quarry	1:15	2.5	4.1	673	205	328	100
3e	Steel Rigg (Once Brewed Exit)	1:45	3.2	5.2	673	205	686	209
3d	Housesteads	1:30	2.3	3.7	427	130	522	159
3c	Grindon exit	0:45	2.1	3.4	62	19	82	25
3b	Carraw B&B	1:15	2.4	3.8	180	55	279	85
3a	Green Carts Farm exit	1:30	2.7	4.3	98	30	571	174
2e	Chollerford	0:15	0.9	1.5	52	16	16	5
2d	Wall exit	2:30	5.6	9	558	170	492	150
2c	Halton Red House	1:30	3.3	5.3	164	50	302	92
2b	Robin Hood Inn	1:30	3.5	5.7	262	80	341	104
2a	Ironsign	1:00	2.4	3.9	213	65	180	55
1c	Heddon-on-the-Wall	1:30	3.6	5.8	66	20	427	130
1b	Newburn	2:45	6.7	10.7	148	45	184	56
1a	Newcastle Swing Bridge	2:00	5.1	8.2	98	30	72	22
Finish	Wallsend							

Suggested Itineraries: East to West

Sunset at Black Carts (Stage 3a)

9 Days (E-W)

This is our most relaxed approach which allows plenty of time to visit all the museums and sites of Hadrian's Wall and to enjoy a lunchtime pint at the many pubs along the way.

Day	Stages	Time (hr)	Distance		Ascent		Descent	
			miles	km	ft	m	ft	m
1	1a, 1b	4:45	11.7	18.9	256	78	246	75
2	1c, 2a, 2b	4.00	9.6	15.4	948	289	541	165
3	2c, 2d	4.00	8.9	14.3	794	242	722	220
4	2e, 3a, 3b, 3c	3:45	8.1	13.0	948	289	394	120
5	3d, 3e, 4a	4:30	8.1	13.0	1536	468	1772	540
6	4b, 4c, 4d	4:45	10.9	17.5	1345	410	1591	485
7	4e, 5a, 5b, 5c, 5d	4.00	9.3	14.9	476	145	886	270
8	5e, 6a	4.00	10.1	16.3	262	80	230	70
9	6b, 6c, 6d, 6e	4.00	10.1	16.2	148	45	213	65

8 Days (E-W)

Days 3 to 8 of the 9-day itinerary are squeezed into five days. The pace is slightly faster but there is still plenty of time to spend at the unmissable forts.

Day	Stages	Time (hr)	Distance		Ascent		Descent	
			miles	km	ft	m	ft	m
1	1a, 1b	4:45	11.7	18.9	256	78	246	75
2	1c, 2a, 2b	4.00	9.6	15.4	948	289	541	165
3	2c, 2d, 2e	4:15	9.8	15.8	810	247	774	236
4	3a, 3b, 3c, 3d	5.00	9.4	15.2	1453	443	768	234
5	3e, 4a, 4b, 4c	5:30	11.8	19.0	1857	566	2412	735
6	4d, 4e, 5a, 5b	4:30	10.0	16.1	978	298	1247	380
7	5c, 5d, 5e, 6a	5:45	14.2	22.9	262	80	394	120
8	6b, 6c, 6d, 6e	4.00	10.1	16.2	148	45	213	65

7 Days (E-W)

The last six days of the 8-day itinerary are squeezed into five days. The first half of the trek is comparatively easier than the second half, allowing you time to warm up before the more difficult central sections.

Day	Stages	Time (hr)	Distance		Ascent		Descent	
			miles	km	ft	m	ft	m
1	1a, 1b	4:45	11.7	18.9	256	78	246	75
2	1c, 2a, 2b	4.00	9.6	15.4	948	289	541	165
3	2c, 2d, 2e, 3a	5:45	12.5	20.1	1381	421	873	266
4	3b, 3c, 3d, 3e	5:15	10.0	16.1	1568	478	1342	409
5	4a, 4b, 4c, 4d, 4e	6:30	14.5	23.3	1795	547	2543	775
6	5a, 5b, 5c, 5d, 5e	5:30	13.3	21.4	354	108	607	185
7	6a, 6b, 6c, 6d, 6e	6.00	15.1	24.3	410	125	443	135

6 Days (E-W)

Our standard schedule which successfully divides up the trek into long but manageable stages. It is a well-balanced approach which is suitable for many walkers.

Day	Stages	Time (hr)	Distance		Ascent		Descent	
			miles	km	ft	m	ft	m
1	1a, 1b, 1c	6:15	15.4	24.7	682	208	312	95
2	2a, 2b, 2c, 2d, 2e	6:45	15.8	25.4	1332	406	1250	381
3	3a, 3b, 3c, 3d, 3e	6:45	12.7	20.4	2139	652	1440	439
4	4a, 4b, 4c, 4d, 4e	6:30	14.5	23.3	1795	547	2543	775
5	5a, 5b, 5c, 5d, 5e	5:30	13.3	21.4	354	108	607	185
6	6a, 6b, 6c, 6d, 6e	6.00	15.1	24.3	410	125	443	135

5 Days (E-W)

For fit hikers who like to move quickly. There is more of a focus on hiking than taking in the attractions of HW. The difficulty ramps up significantly and all five days are long. Day 3 in particular is pretty tough.

Day	Stages	Time (hr)	Distance		Ascent		Descent	
			miles	km	ft	m	ft	m
1	1a, 1b, 1c, 2a	7:15	17.8	28.6	863	263	525	160
2	2b, 2c, 2d, 2e, 3a	7:15	16.0	25.8	1723	525	1135	346
3	3b, 3c, 3d, 3e, 4a, 4b	8:15	16.7	26.8	2608	795	2884	879
4	4c, 4d, 4e, 5a, 5b, 5c, 5d	7.00	16.0	25.8	1109	338	1608	490
5	5e, 6a, 6b, 6c, 6d, 6e	8.00	20.2	32.5	410	125	443	135

4 Days (E-W)

A tough itinerary for fit and experienced walkers and runners. The times are based on walking speeds (to enable accurate comparison with the other itineraries) so runners will need to adjust them accordingly.

Day	Stages	Time (hr)	Distance		Ascent		Descent	
			miles	km	ft	m	ft	m
1	1a, 1b, 1c, 2a, 2b	8:45	21.3	34.3	1204	367	787	240
2	2c, 2d, 2e, 3a, 3b, 3c, 3d	9:15	19.3	31.0	2264	690	1542	470
3	3e, 4a, 4b, 4c, 4d, 4e, 5a, 5b	10.00	21.8	35.1	2835	864	3658	1115
4	5c, 5d, 5e, 6a, 6b, 6c, 6d, 6e	9:45	24.3	39.1	410	125	607	185

3 Days (E-W)

A very demanding itinerary for fit and experienced runners. Daily times and distances increase gradually over the three days. The times are based on walking speeds (to enable accurate comparison with the other itineraries) so runners will need to adjust them accordingly.

Day	Stages	Time (hr)	Distance		Ascent		Descent	
			miles	km	ft	m	ft	m
1	1a, 1b, 1c, 2a, 2b, 2c	10:15	24.6	39.6	1506	459	951	290
2	2d, 2e, 3a, 3b, 3c, 3d, 3e, 4a, 4b, 4c	13:15	27.8	44.7	3819	1164	3790	1155
3	4d, 4e, 5a, 5b, 5c, 5d, 5e, 6a, 6b, 6c, 6d, 6e	14:15	34.3	55.2	1388	423	1854	565

Both Broad Wall and Narrow Wall are visible at Planetrees (Stage 2d)

Suggested Itineraries: West to East

A remote part of the NNP (Stage 3b)

9 Days (W-E)

This is our most relaxed approach which allows plenty of time to visit all the museums and sites of HW and to enjoy a lunchtime pint at the many pubs along the way.

Day	Stages	Time (hr)	Distance		Ascent		Descent	
			miles	km	ft	m	ft	m
1	6e, 6d, 6c, 6b	4.00	10.1	16.2	213	65	148	45
2	6a, 5e	4.00	10.1	16.3	230	70	262	80
3	5d, 5c, 5b, 5a	3:30	8.2	13.2	607	185	354	108
4	4e, 4d, 4c	3:30	7.8	12.6	1001	305	755	230
5	4b, 4a, 3e	4:45	9.9	15.9	2215	675	1726	526
6	3d, 3c, 3b, 3a	5.00	9.4	15.2	768	234	1453	443
7	2e, 2d, 2c	4:15	9.8	15.8	774	236	810	247
8	2b, 2a, 1c	4.00	9.6	15.4	541	165	948	289
9	1b, 1a	4:45	11.7	18.9	246	75	256	78

8 Days (W-E)

Days 3 to 8 of the 9-day itinerary are squeezed into five days. The pace is slightly faster but there is still plenty of time to spend at the unmissable forts.

Day	Stages	Time (hr)	Distance		Ascent		Descent	
			miles	km	ft	m	ft	m
1	6e, 6d, 6c, 6b	4.00	10.1	16.2	213	65	148	45
2	6a, 5e	4.00	10.1	16.3	230	70	262	80
3	5d, 5c, 5b, 5a, 4e	4.00	9.3	14.9	886	270	476	145
4	4d, 4c, 4b	4:45	10.9	17.5	1591	485	1345	410
5	4a, 3e, 3d, 3c	5:15	10.2	16.4	1834	559	1618	493
6	3b, 3a, 2e, 2d	5:30	11.6	18.6	889	271	1358	414
7	2c, 2b, 2a, 1c	5:30	12.9	20.7	705	215	1250	381
8	1b, 1a	4:45	11.7	18.9	246	75	256	78

7 Days (W-E)

Days 2 to 6 of the 8-day itinerary are squeezed into four days. The first three days allow time to warm up before the more difficult central sections.

Day	Stages	Time (hr)	Distance		Ascent		Descent	
			miles	km	ft	m	ft	m
1	6e, 6d, 6c, 6b	4.00	10.1	16.2	213	65	148	45
2	6a, 5e, 5d, 5c	5:45	14.2	22.9	394	120	262	80
3	5b, 5a, 4e, 4d, 4c	5:15	11.9	19.2	1444	440	1109	338
4	4b, 4a, 3e, 3d	6:15	12.2	19.6	2641	805	2247	685
5	3c, 3b, 3a, 2e, 2d	6:15	13.7	22.0	951	290	1440	439
6	2c, 2b, 2a, 1c	5:30	12.9	20.7	705	215	1250	381
7	1b, 1a	4:45	11.7	18.9	246	75	256	78

6 Days (W-E)

Our standard schedule which successfully divides up the trek into long but manageable stages. It is a well-balanced approach which is suitable for many walkers.

Day	Stages	Time (hr)	Distance		Ascent		Descent	
			miles	km	ft	m	ft	m
1	6e, 6d, 6c, 6b, 6a	6.00	15.1	24.3	443	135	410	125
2	5e, 5d, 5c, 5b, 5a	5:30	13.3	21.4	607	185	354	108
3	4e, 4d, 4c, 4b, 4a	6:30	14.5	23.3	2543	775	1795	547
4	3e, 3d, 3c, 3b, 3a	6:45	12.7	20.4	1440	439	2139	652
5	2e, 2d, 2c, 2b, 2a	6:45	15.8	25.4	1250	381	1332	406
6	1c, 1b, 1a	6:15	15.4	24.7	312	95	682	208

5 Days (W-E)

For fit hikers who like to move quickly. There is more of a focus on hiking than taking in the attractions of HW. The difficulty ramps up significantly and all five days are long. Days 2 and 4 in particular are tough.

Day	Stages	Time (hr)	Distance		Ascent		Descent	
			miles	km	ft	m	ft	m
1	6e, 6d, 6c, 6b, 6a	6.0	15.1	24.3	443	135	410	125
2	5e, 5d, 5c, 5b, 5a, 4e, 4d	8:15	18.1	29.2	1411	430	978	298
3	4c, 4b, 4a, 3e, 3d, 3c	7:45	16.2	26.1	2900	884	2461	750
4	3b, 3a, 2e, 2d, 2c, 2b	8:30	18.4	29.6	1316	401	2001	610
5	2a, 1c, 1b, 1a	7:15	17.8	28.6	525	160	863	263

4 Days (W-E)

A tough itinerary for fit and experienced walkers and runners. The times are based on walking speeds (to enable accurate comparison with the other itineraries) so runners will need to adjust them accordingly.

Day	Stages	Time (hr)	Distance		Ascent		Descent	
			miles	km	ft	m	ft	m
1	6e, 6d, 6c, 6b, 6a, 5e	8.00	20.2	32.5	443	135	410	125
2	5d, 5c, 5b, 5a, 4e, 4d, 4c, 4b	8:45	20.1	32.4	2477	755	1821	555
3	4a, 3e, 3d, 3c, 3b, 3a, 2e, 2d	10:45	21.8	35.0	2723	830	2976	907
4	2c, 2b, 2a, 1c, 1b, 1a	10:15	24.6	39.6	951	290	1506	459

3 Days (W-E)

A very demanding itinerary for fit and experienced runners. Daily times and distances increase gradually over the three days. The times are based on walking speeds (to enable accurate comparison with the other itineraries) so runners will need to adjust them accordingly.

Day	Stages	Time (hr)	Distance		Ascent		Descent	
			miles	km	ft	m	ft	m
1	6e, 6d, 6c, 6b, 6a, 5e, 5d, 5c	9:45	24.3	39.1	607	185	410	125
2	5b, 5a, 4e, 4d, 4c, 4b, 4a, 3e, 3d, 3c, 3b	13:30	28.6	46.0	4328	1319	3717	1133
3	3a, 2e, 2d, 2c, 2b, 2a, 1c, 1b, 1a	14:30	33.8	54.4	1660	506	2585	788

Poltross Burn Milecastle (Stage 4d)

Accommodation

Robin Hood Inn (Stage 2b/2c)

The HWP is a popular trek and there is a wide range of accommodation including 'bed and breakfasts', pubs, hotels, hostels, bunkhouses and camping barns. Accommodation listings are provided on pages 24-33: there are so many places to stay in the region that it is not possible to list all of them. All contact details were correct at the date of press but be aware that this information frequently changes. Please let us know about any changes. For camping, see page 22.

These days, most people have their entire trip booked before they depart. The recent rise in the number of companies offering unguided trips means that an increasing number of HWP beds are block-booked months in advance. This makes it harder for the independent trekker to secure the best accommodation unless booked well in advance.

In July/August and during other school holidays, the trail is very busy and forward booking is normally essential. You might get lucky and be able to cobble together a set of bookings at the last minute but you are unlikely to get 'first-choice' accommodation right next to the trail.

Even outside of July/August, it is wise to book ahead, particularly at weekends and on stages where there is only one place to stay. That said, in April, May, June, September and October, it is still perfectly possible for the independent trekker to get last-minute bookings, particularly if you can be flexible with dates and places and are prepared to stay in towns/villages a few miles away from the HWP. The accommodation right next to the HWP books up most quickly. As you move further away from the trail, bookings are often easier to secure. Many places will be willing to pick you up from the trail and leave you back the next morning. Alternatively, there are many local taxi companies who will pick you up for a very reasonable price: see 'Public Transport along Hadrian's Wall'.

In April (excluding Easter) and October, fewer people walk the route so there is less demand for accommodation: in these months, you can often still get away with booking only a day or two in advance. However, you can get caught out if, for example, a large group has booked up a lot of beds. Before April, and from November onwards, some accommodation may be closed so check in advance. For more booking tips, see page 33.

Bed & Breakfasts (B&Bs):

these form the back-bone of HWP accommodation. Traditionally, they were private homes which offered rooms and breakfast to visitors. Nowadays, however, you find many bigger and more professionally run properties. Bed and breakfast normally costs £35-50 per person sharing a double/twin room. Rates for solo travellers are usually higher because they pay a single occupancy rate. Normally, the ensuite bedrooms are basic but clean and comfortable. 'Full English' breakfast is the norm: a large helping of bacon, sausage, eggs, mushrooms and black pudding. Most do not provide evening meals but the owner should be able to recommend a local pub or restaurant. Most B&Bs have their own websites and many list their rooms on one of the generic travel booking sites such as expedia.com or booking.com.

Pubs & Inns:

most villages have a pub and many of them offer bed and breakfast accommodation. This normally costs £35-50 per person sharing a double/twin room. Rates for solo travellers are usually higher because they pay a single occupancy rate. Evening meals are usually available and the standard of food these days is fairly high. Most of the pubs serve a selection of the excellent cask ales for which England is famous: for some, this is a highlight of the HWP. Most pubs have their own websites.

Hotels:

the hotels on offer range from basic ones to more luxury properties. Prices vary widely. They all provide 'Full English' breakfast and most also offer evening meals. Most hotels have their own websites and many list their rooms on one of the generic travel booking sites such as expedia.com or booking.com.

Hostels:

these offer beds in dormitories and sometimes private rooms. Generally, they will have shared bathrooms, self-catering kitchen facilities and communal areas. Continental breakfast (tea and toast) is sometimes available. Bedding is usually supplied. Like B&Bs, hostels are becoming more upmarket and prices rise along with the quality of the offering. A bed usually costs £20-30 per person. Groups of two or more may find B&Bs to be better value.

Bunkhouses & camping barns:

these are dormitories at farms, country houses or hotels. Quality varies and often the accommodation is very basic. Usually, there will be showers and self-catering facilities but often you will need to bring your own sleeping bag. Prices are low.

The Sill YHA at Once Brewed (Stage 3e/4a)

Camping

Chesters Fort was strategically placed to overlook the River North Tyne (Stage 3a)

Camping is the cheapest way to hike the HWP: a pitch each night costs £7-10 per person. It also offers more freedom because campsites rarely need to be booked far in advance and you can normally adjust your itinerary as you go. Wild camping is not permitted on the HWP so campers must stay in the privately-owned campsites along the route. There are campsites on most parts of the trail, however, there are none E of the Robin Hood Inn (Stage 2b/2c): this means that campers have a very long first or last day (depending on direction of travel) so many prefer to break up this section by staying in a B&B or pub. To help campers plan, a list of campsites is set out below: contact details and information on the facilities are set out in the full Accommodation Listings (see pages 24-33).

Normally campsites are clean and well-maintained. Frequently, they are part of a farm and can be some of the loveliest places to spend the night. Showers are normally provided but you may pay a little extra for this luxury. During the school holidays in July/August, it can be a good idea to book in advance. Otherwise, you should not need to book far ahead. However, it is always sensible to telephone at least a day or two before so the campsite knows to expect you.

The obvious downside to camping is that you need to carry a lot more gear: tents, sleeping mats, sleeping bags and stoves all add weight to your pack, making the trek more difficult. However, this could be alleviated by using a baggage transfer service to transfer your heavy bags between campsites (see 'Baggage transfer').

Stage	Campsite
Stage 2b/2c	Robin Hood Inn
Stage 2c (1 mile off-route)	Well House Farm Campsite
Stage 2d Acomb (2-3 miles off-route)	Fallowfield Dene Campsite
Stage 2e/3a Chollerford	Riverside Campsite
Stage 3a/3b	Green Carts Campsite & Bunkhouse
Stage 3e/4a Once Brewed	Winshields Campsite
Stage 4a (0.8 miles S of Caw Gap)	Hadrian's Wall Campsite
Stage 4a (1 mile S of Cawfields Quarry)	Herding Hill Farm Campsite
Stage 4b/4c	Holmhead Guest House
Stage 4d/4e Banks	Quarryside Campsite
Stage 5b	Sandysike Bunkhouse & Camping
Stage 5c (1 mile off-route)	Stonewalls Campsite
Stage 5c/5d	Bleatarn Farm Campsite
Stage 5d/5e	Crosby Camping
Stage 6a/6b Beaumont	Roman Wall Lodges
Stage 6b/6c Boustead Hill	Highfield Farm B&B

Sycamore Gap (Stage 3e)

Accommodation Listings

🛏 Dormitory/Bunkhouse
🛎 Private Room
⛰ Camping
🍷 Drinks
🥪 Lunch
🍴 Evening Meals
🥐 Breakfast
🛒 Food shop
📶 WiFi

Stage	Name	Facilities	Contact Details
1a	Crocket's Hotel	🛎 📶 🍷 🥐 🥪 🍴	0191 262 3010 Book at www.booking.com
1a/1b Newcastle	Premier Inn Quayside	🛎 📶 🍷 🥐 🥪 🍴	0333 321 1347 www.premierinn.com
1a/1b Newcastle	Travelodge Newcastle Quayside	🛎 📶 🍷 🥐 🥪 🍴	08719 846524 www.travelodge.co.uk
1a/1b Newcastle	Vermont Hotel	🛎 📶 🍷 🥐 🥪 🍴	0191 233 1010 info@vermonthotel.co.uk www.vermont-hotel.com
1a/1b Newcastle	Malmaison Hotel	🛎 📶 🍷 🥐 🥪 🍴	0191 389 8627 www.malmaison.com
1a/1b Newcastle	Sleeperz Hotel	🛎 📶 🍷 🥐 🥪 🍴	0191 261 6171 reservationsnewcastle@sleeperz.com www.sleeperz.com
1a/1b Newcastle	County Hotel	🛎 📶 🍷 🥐 🥪 🍴	0191 232 2471 reception@countyhotel.co.uk www.countyhotel.co.uk
1a/1b Newcastle	Royal Station Hotel	🛎 📶 🍷 🥐 🥪 🍴	0191 232 0781 info@royalstationhotel.com www.royalstationhotel.com
1a/1b Newcastle	Copthorne Hotel	🛎 📶 🍷 🥐 🥪 🍴	0191 222 0333 sales.newcastle@millenniumhotels.com www.millenniumhotels.com

Stage	Name	Facilities	Contact Details
1a/1b Newcastle	YHA Newcastle Central	🛏 🔒 📶 🍷 🥐 🍴	0345 260 2583 newcastlecentral@yha.org.uk www.yha.org.uk
1a/1b Newcastle	Albatross Hostel	🛏 🔒 📶	0191 233 1330 info@albatrossnewcastle.co.uk www.albatrossnewcastle.co.uk
1b/1c Newburn	Keelman's Lodge	🔒 📶 🍷 🥐 🍔 🍴	0191 267 1689 www.keelmanslodge.co.uk
1c/2a Heddon-on-the-Wall	Heddon Lodge	🔒 📶 🍷 🥐	01661 854 042 07802 660 485 info@heddonlodge.co.uk www.heddonlodge.co.uk
1c/2a Heddon-on-the-Wall	Hadrian's Barn	🔒 📶 🥐	07944 004 601 info@hadriansbarn.co.uk www.hadriansbarn.co.uk
1c/2a Heddon-on-the-Wall	Houghton North Farm Hostel	🔒 🛏 🥐	01661 854 364 07708 419911 bookings@ hadrianswallaccommodation.com www.houghtonnorthfarm.co.uk
1c/2a Wylam (off-route)	The Ship Inn	🔒 📶 🍷 🥐 🍔 🍴	01661 854 538 info@theshipwylam.co.uk www.theshipinnwylam.co.uk
1c/2a Wylam (off-route)	Black Bull Inn	🔒 📶 🍷 🥐 🍔 🍴	01661 853 112
1c/2a Wylam (off-route)	The Boathouse Pub	🔒 📶 🍷 🥐 🍔 🍴	01661 853 431
1c/2a Wylam (off-route)	Wormald House B&B	🔒 📶 🥐 Free pick-up from Heddon	07815 903167 07850 322406 stay@wormaldhouse.co.uk www.wormaldhouse.co.uk
Stage 2a/2b	Ironsign Farm B&B	🔒 📶 🥐	01661 853 802 lowen532@aol.com
Stage 2b (½ mile off-route)	Northside Farm Wigwams	🔒	07904 119 327 info@northsidefarm.co.uk www.northsidefarm.co.uk
Stage 2b/2c	Robin Hood Inn	🔒 ⛺ 🍷 🥐 🍔 🍴	01434 672 549 robinhood_northumberland@ outlook.com www.robinhoodinnhadrianswall.com

Stage	Name	Facilities	Contact Details
Stage 2c (1 mile off-route)	Matfen High House B&B	🔒🔑 📶 🥐	01661 886 592 jennymatfenhh@gmail.com
Stage 2c (1 mile off-route)	Dark Sky Glamping	🔒🔑 🍷 🥐 🍔 🍴	relax@darkskyglamping.co.uk www.darkskyglamping.co.uk
Stage 2c (1 mile off-route)	Well House Farm Campsite	⛺	07817 858178 07811 712770 info@wellhousefarm.co.uk www.wellhousefarm.co.uk
Stage 2c/2d	Halton Red House B&B	🔒🔑 📶 🥐	01434 672 209
Stage 2d Corbridge (2-3 miles off-route)	The Angel of Corbridge pub	🔒🔑 📶 🍷 🥐 🍔 🍴	01434 632119 info@theangelofcorbridge.com www.theangelofcorbridge.com
Stage 2d Corbridge (2-3 miles off-route)	The Wheatsheaf Hotel	🔒🔑 📶 🍷 🥐 🍔 🍴	01434 409 588 enquiries@ thewheatsheafcorbridge.co.uk www.thewheatsheafcorbridge.co.uk
Stage 2d Corbridge (2-3 miles off-route)	The Golden Lion Pub	🔒🔑 📶 🍷 🥐 🍔 🍴	01434 634 507 amyfox93@gmail.com www.goldenlioncorbridge.co.uk
Stage 2d Corbridge (2-3 miles off-route)	Peartree House B&B	🔒🔑 🥐	01434 632 223 contactus@ peartreebedandbreakfast.com www.peartreebedandbreakfast.com
Stage 2d Corbridge (2-3 miles off-route)	Norgate B&B	🔒🔑 📶 🥐	01434 633 736 welcome@norgatecorbridge.co.uk www.norgatecorbridge.co.uk
Stage 2d Corbridge (2-3 miles off-route)	Dyvels Inn	🔒🔑 📶 🍷 🥐 🍔 🍴	01434 632 888 thedyvelscorbridge@gmail.com www.thedyvelsinn.com
Stage 2d Acomb (2-3 miles off-route)	The Sun Inn	🔒🔑 📶 🍷 🥐	01434 602 934
Stage 2d Acomb (2-3 miles off-route)	Fallowfield Dene Campsite	⛺ 🍷 🛒	01434 603 553 www.fallowfielddene.co.uk
Stage 2d Acomb (2-3 miles off-route)	The Queen's Arms	🔒🔑 📶 🍷 🥐 🍔 🍴	01434 607857 www.the-queens-arms-hotel.business.site

Stage	Name	Facilities	Contact Details
Stage 2d Hexham (4.5 miles off-route)	The Station Inn	🔒📶🍷🥧🍔🍴	01434 603 155
Stage 2d Hexham (4.5 miles off-route)	Beaumont Hotel	🔒📶🍷🥧🍔🍴	01434 602 331 reservations@ thebeaumonthexham.co.uk www.thebeaumonthexham.co.uk
Stage 2d Hexham (4.5 miles off-route)	The County Hotel	🔒📶🍷🥧🍔🍴	01434 608 444 countyhotelcontact@gmail.com www.countyhotelhexham.co.uk
Stage 2d Hexham (4.5 miles off-route)	Hexham Town B&B	🔒📶🥧	07714 292 602 Hexhamtownbandb@gmail.com hexhamtownbedandbreakfast.co.uk
Stage 2d Hexham (4.5 miles off-route)	Tap & Spile	🔒📶🍷🥧🍔🍴	0191 816 0356 hexhamtap@gmail.com
Stage 2d Hexham (4.5 miles off-route)	Bridge House B&B	🔒📶🥧	01434 609 973 relax@bridgehousehexham.co.uk www.bridgehousehexham.co.uk
Stage 2d/2e Wall	The Hadrian Hotel	🔒📶🍷🥧🍔🍴	01434 681 232 manager@hadrianhotel.co.uk www.hadrianhotel.co.uk
Stage 2e/3a Chollerford	The George Hotel	🔒📶🍷🥧🍔🍴	Closed at the date of press
Stage 2e/3a Chollerford	Chesters Bridge B&B	🔒📶🥧	01434 689856 www.chestersbridge.co.uk
Stage 2e/3a Chollerford	Riverside Campsite	⛺	01434 681 325 01434 689 850 info@theriversidekitchen.co.uk
Humshaugh (0.6 miles N of Chollerford)	Orchard View B&B	🔒📶🥧	01434 681 658 northumberlandbedandbreakfast.biz
Stage 3a (off-route)	The Dovecote B&B	🔒📶🥧	01434 681 984/07851 001 337 jane@dovecotehadrianswall.co.uk www.dovecotehadrianswall.co.uk
Stage 3a	Walwick Hall Hotel	🔒📶🍷🥧🍔🍴	01434 620 156 hello@walwickhall.com www.walwickhall.com

Stage	Name	Facilities	Contact Details
Stage 3a/3b	Green Carts Campsite & Bunkhouse	Takeaway food can be ordered	01434 681 320 www.greencarts.co.uk
Stage 3b (1.5 miles off-route)	Hallbarns B&B		01434 681 419 enquiries@hallbarns-simonburn.co.uk www.hallbarns-simonburn.co.uk
Stage 3b/3c	Carraw B&B		01434 689 857 relax@carraw.co.uk www.carraw.co.uk
Stage 3c/3d Grindon	The Old Repeater Station		01434 688 668 les.gibson@tiscali.co.uk hadrians-wall-bedandbreakfast.co.uk
Stage 3d/3e Housesteads	Beggar Bog B&B		beggarbog@gmail.com www.beggarbog.co.uk
Stage 3e/4a Once Brewed	YHA The Sill		0345 260 2702 thesill@yha.org.uk www.yha.org.uk
Stage 3e/4a Once Brewed	The Twice Brewed Inn & Microbrewery		01434 344 534 contact@twicebrewedinn.co.uk www.twicebrewedinn.co.uk
Stage 3e/4a Once Brewed	Vallum Lodge B&B		01434 344 248 stay@vallum-lodge.co.uk www.vallum-lodge.co.uk
Stage 3e/4a Once Brewed	Winshields Campsite		07968 102 780 malcolm@winshieldscampsite.co.uk www.winshieldscampsite.co.uk
Stage 4a (0.8 miles S of Caw Gap)	Hadrian's Wall Campsite		01434 320 495 info@hadrianswallcampsite.co.uk www.hadrianswallcampsite.co.uk
Stage 4a/4b (½ mile S of Cawfields Quarry)	Bridge House B&B		01434 320 744 info@bridgehousecawfields.co.uk www.bridgehousecawfields.co.uk
Stage 4a/4b (1 mile S of Cawfields Quarry)	Herding Hill Farm Campsite		01434 320 175 bookings@herdinghillfarm.co.uk www.herdinghillfarm.co.uk
Stage 4a/4b Haltwhistle (3 miles off-route)	The Grey Bull B&B		01434 321 991 07875 480 225 hello@greybullhotel.co.uk www.greybullhotel.co.uk

Stage	Name	Facilities	Contact Details
Stage 4a/4b Haltwhistle (3 miles off-route)	Ashcroft Guest House	🔑 📶 🥧	01434 320 213 07739 183 847 info@ashcroftguesthouse.co.uk www.ashcroftguesthouse.co.uk
Stage 4a/4b Haltwhistle (3 miles off-route)	Manor House Inn	🔑 📶 🍷 🥧 🍔 🍴 Free shuttle to/from HWP	01434 322 588 welcome@manorhousehaltwhistle.com www.manorhousehaltwhistle.com
Stage 4a/4b Haltwhistle (3 miles off-route)	Centre of Britain Hotel	🔑 📶 🍷 🥧 🍴	01434 322 422 manager@centre-of-britain.org.uk www.centreofbritain.co.uk
Stage 4a/4b Haltwhistle (3 miles off-route)	Belford House	🔑	01434 322 572 info@belfordhouserooms.co.uk www.belfordhouserooms.co.uk
Stage 4a/4b Haltwhistle (3 miles off-route)	The Old School House B&B	🔑 📶 🥧	01434 312 013 07792 270 262 office@oldschoolhousehaltwhistle.com www.oldschoolhousehaltwhistle.com
Stage 4a/4b Haltwhistle (3 miles off-route)	Chare Close B&B	🔑 🥧	07881 103 148 chareclosebandb@gmail.com www.chareclose.com
Stage 4b	Walltown Lodge B&B	🔑 📶 🥧	07415 058 350 walltownlodge@hotmail.com www.walltownlodge.co.uk
Stage 4b/4c	Holmhead Guest House	🔑 🛏 ⛺ 🥧	01697 747 402 holmhead@forestbarn.com www.bandb-hadrianswall.co.uk
Stage 4c Greenhead (0.4 miles off-route)	Greenhead Hotel	🔑 📶 🍷 🥧 🍔 🍴	01697 747 411 info@greenheadbrampton.co.uk www.greenheadbrampton.co.uk
Stage 4c Greenhead (0.4 miles off-route)	Greenhead Hostel	🛏 🥧	01697 747 411 info@greenheadbrampton.co.uk www.greenheadbrampton.co.uk
Stage 4c (0.4 miles off-route)	Hadrian's Holiday Lodges B&B	🔑 🥧	01697 747 972 www.hadriansholidays.com
Stage 4c/4d Gilsland	The Samson Inn	🔑 📶 🍷 🥧 🍔 🍴	01697 747 962 info@thesamson.co.uk www.thesamson.co.uk

29

Stage	Name	Facilities	Contact Details
Stage 4c/4d Gilsland	Brookside Villa B&B	🔒 📶 🍷 🥐 🍴	01697 747 300 info@brooksidevilla.com www.brooksidevilla.com
Stage 4c/4d Gilsland	Hollies On The Wall	🔒 📶 🥐	01697 747 267/07552 234 290 jackie@theholliesonthewall.co.uk www.theholliesonthewall.co.uk
Stage 4c/4d Gilsland	Hill on the Wall B&B	🔒 📶 🥐	01697 747 214 info@hillonthewall.co.uk www.hillonthewall.co.uk
Stage 4c/4d Gilsland	Brooklands B&B	🔒 📶 🥐	01697 747 168 info@brooklandsuk.com www.brooklandsuk.com
Stage 4d	Willowford Farm	🔒 📶	01697 747 962 stay@willowford.co.uk www.willowford.co.uk
Stage 4d (0.6 miles off-route)	Slack House Farm	🛏 🔒 🥐 🍴 🛒	01697 747 351 slackhouseorganicfarm@gmail.com www.slackhousefarm.co.uk
Stage 4d/4e Banks	Quarryside Campsite	⛺	07838 225108/01697 72538 campingatbanks@gmail.com www.quarryside.co.uk
Stage 4e	Haytongate Barn	🔒 📶	01697 741 119/ 01697 741 797 mike@geltgifts.co.uk www.haytongate.com
Stage 4e/5a Lanercost (½ mile off-route)	Abbey Farmhouse B&B	🔒 📶 🍷 🥐 🍴	01697 73148 info@abbeyfarmhouse.com www.abbeyfarmhouse.com
Stage 5a/5b Walton	Florries on the Wall	🛏 🔒 🥐 🍷 🍴	www.florriesonthewall.co.uk
Stage 5a/5b Walton	Low Rigg Farm B&B	🔒 📶 🥐	01697 73233 annt22.at@gmail.com www.lowriggfarm.co.uk
Stage 5a/5b Walton	Old Vicarage Brewery	🔒 📶 🍷 🥐 🍴	01697 543 002 tythinggraham@aol.com www.oldvicaragebrewery.co.uk
Stage 5a/5b Walton	Greenacres B&B	🔒 📶 🥐	07747 463233 info@greenacreswalton.co.uk www.greenacreswalton.co.uk
Stage 5b	Sandysike Bunkhouse & Camping	🛏 ⛺ 📶 🥐 🍴	07725 645 929 01697 507 067 sandysike@gmx.com
Stage 5b	Headswood on the Wall	🔒 📶	07866 395 731 info@headswoodonthewall.co.uk www.headswoodonthewall.co.uk

Stage	Name	Facilities	Contact Details
Stage 5b/5c Newtown	Orchard House B&B	🔒 📶 🥧 Transport to local pub on request	01697 742 637 07774 078 173 orchardhouse1783@yahoo.com www.orchardhousebednb.co.uk
Stage 5b/5c Newtown	Hadrian's Wall Studio (at the Snack Shed)	🔒 📶 🥧	Book at www.booking.com
Stage 5b/5c Brampton (2.5 miles off-route)	The Howard Arms	🔒 📶 🍸 🥧 🍔 🍴	01697 742 758 www.howardarmsbrampton.co.uk
Stage 5b/5c Brampton (2.5 miles off-route)	Scotch Arms Mews B&B	🔒 📶 🥧	07786 115 621 info@thescotcharmsmews.co.uk www.thescotcharmsmews.co.uk
Stage 5b/5c Brampton (2.5 miles off-route)	Oakwood Park Hotel	🔒 📶 🍸 🥧 🍴	01697 72436 donald@oakwoodparkhotel.co.uk www.oakwoodparkhotel.co.uk
Stage 5c (1 mile off-route)	Stonewalls Campsite	⛺	01228 573 666
Stage 5c/5d	Bleatarn Farm Campsite	⛺	07795 490 579
Stage 5d/5e	Crosby Camping	⛺	01228 573000 info@crosbycamping.co.uk
Stage 5e (0.3 miles off-route)	Park Broom Lodge	🔒 📶 🍸 🥧 🍔 🍴	01228 573696 info@parkbroomlodge.co.uk www.parkbroomlodge.co.uk
Stage 5e/6a Carlisle	Ashleigh Guest House	🔒 📶 🥧	01228 521 631 info@ashleighbedandbreakfast.co.uk www.ashleighbedandbreakfast.co.uk
Stage 5e/6a Carlisle	Abberley House B&B	🔒 📶 🥧	01228 521 645 info@abberleyhouse.co.uk www.abberleyhouse.co.uk
Stage 5e/6a Carlisle	Cartref Guest House	🔒 📶 🥧	01228 522 077 cartrefguest@gmail.com www.cartrefguesthouse.co.uk
Stage 5e/6a Carlisle	Crown & Mitre Hotel	🔒 📶 🍸 🥧 🍔 🍴	01228 525 491 www.peelhotels.co.uk
Stage 5e/6a Carlisle	Cornerways B&B	🔒 📶 🥧	01228 521 733 info@cornerwaysbandb.co.uk www.cornerwaysbandb.co.uk
Stage 5e/6a Carlisle	Travelodge Carlisle Centre	🔒 📶 🍸 🥧 🍴	08719 846 374 www.travelodge.co.uk

Stage	Name	Facilities	Contact Details
Stage 5e/6a Carlisle	The County Hotel	🔒🔑 📶 🍷 🥧 🍔 🍴	01228 531 316 www.countycarlisle.com
Stage 5e/6a Carlisle	Ibis Carlisle City Centre Hotel	🔒🔑 📶 🍷 🥧 🍔 🍴	01228 587 690 H3443@accor.com www.all.accor.com
Stage 5e/6a Carlisle	Carlisle City Hostel	🔒🔑 🛏️ 📶 🥧	07914 720 821 info@carlislecityhostel.com www.carlislecityhostel.com
Stage 5e/6a Carlisle	Langleigh Guest House	🔒🔑 📶 🥧	01228 530 440/07810 456 650 langleighhouse@aol.com www.langleighhouse.co.uk
Stage 5e/6a Carlisle	Howard Lodge Guest House	🔒🔑 📶 🥧	01228 529 842 www.howard-lodge.co.uk
Stage 5e/6a Carlisle	Warwick Lodge Guest House	🔒🔑 📶 🥧	01228 523 796 warwicklodge112@gmail.com www.warwicklodgecarlisle.co.uk
Stage 5e/6a Carlisle	Townhouse B&B	🔒🔑 📶 🥧	01228 598 782 enquiries@townhousebandb.com www.townhousebandb.com
Stage 5e/6a Carlisle	Fern Lee Guest House	🔒🔑 📶 🥧	01228 511 930 info@fernleeguesthouse.co.uk www.fernleeguesthouse.co.uk
Stage 6a/6b Beaumont	Roman Wall Lodges	⛺ 🔒🔑 🥧	07784 736 423 enquiries@romanwall-lodges.co.uk hadrians-wall-accommodation.co.uk
Stage 6b/6c Boustead Hill	Highfield Farm B&B	⛺ 🔒🔑 🥧	01228 576 060/07976 170 538 info@highfield-holidays.co.uk www.highfield-holidays.co.uk
Stage 6b/6c Boustead Hill	Hillside Farm B&B Bunk Barn	🔒🔑 🛏️ 📶 🥧	01228 576 398 www.hadrianswalkbnb.co.uk
Stage 6c (0.3 miles off-route)	Midtown Farm B&B	🔒🔑 📶 🥧	01228 576 550/ 07967 406 937 janice@midtown-farm.co.uk www.midtown-farm.co.uk
Stage 6c/6d Glasson	Highland Laddie Inn	🔒🔑 📶 🍷 🥧 🍔 🍴	Closed at the date of press
Stage 6d/6e Port Carlisle	Hope & Anchor pub	🔒🔑 🍷 🥧 🍔 🍴	016973 51460 hopeandanchor@mail.com www.hopeandanchor.webador.co.uk
Stage 6e Bowness-on-Solway	Shore Gate House B&B	🔒🔑 📶 🥧	016973 51308 bookings@shoregatehouse.co.uk www.shoregatehouse.co.uk

Stage	Name	Facilities	Contact Details
Stage 6e Bowness-on-Solway	Bowness House Farm	🎒 📶 🥧 🍷 🍰 🍴	016973 52418 07873 200 997 hunterstella@rocketmail.com bownesshousefarmholidaycomplex.co.uk
Stage 6e Bowness-on-Solway	Wallsend Guest House & Glamping Pods	🎒 📶 🥧 ⛺	016973 51055 info@thewallsend.co.uk www.thewallsend.co.uk
Stage 6e Bowness-on-Solway	Lindow Hall Bunkroom	🛏 🥧	01228 576157 bookings@lindowhall.org.uk www.lindowhall.org.uk

HWP Booking Tips

▶ The HWP becomes more popular each year. To ensure that you secure your accommodation of choice, book as early as you can. Many trekkers start booking in autumn (just after the current summer season has ended) for the following season.

▶ Try to book 'hot-spots' first: generally these are places where there are only a few accommodation options. Once you have secured the accommodation which books up most quickly, you can normally slot in the rest of your accommodation more easily. If you leave hot-spots until last then you might have to unwind and rebook other reservations if any hot-spots that you desire are unavailable.

▶ Start mid-week. A large number of trekkers start the trail at the weekend. Those who start mid-week are often 'out of sync' with the bulk of the trekkers and may therefore find accommodation more easily.

▶ Weekends are normally busier (even in low season).

▶ If you cannot get accommodation along the HWP itself, try looking for beds in towns and villages a few miles away.

▶ Accommodation with private rooms usually books up most quickly. If you are prepared to stay in the dormitories at bunkhouses and camping barns then you should find a bed more easily.

▶ Those who hike alone, or in pairs, will find it easiest to find beds. For larger groups, it is more difficult.

▶ If you cannot secure the accommodation that you need then contact one of the unguided tour companies or accommodation booking services. They block-book accommodation months in advance and may have spaces.

▶ Occasionally, the last minute booker can get lucky: tour companies which pre-book in blocks will release unsold beds a few weeks or months before the dates. If you call a few weeks before your trip, you may be lucky enough to bag some beds which have just been released.

Facilities

Stage	Place	Dormitory Beds	Private Rooms	Camping	Meals/Drinks	Food Shop	Transport
1a/1b	Newcastle	✓	✓		✓	✓	train, bus
1b/1c	Newburn		✓		✓		bus
1c/2a	Heddon-on-the-Wall		✓		✓	✓	bus
1c/2a (off-route)	Wylam	✓	✓		✓	✓	
2a/2b	Ironsign		✓		✓		
2b/2c	Robin Hood Inn		✓	✓	✓		
2c/2d	Halton Red House		✓		✓		
Stage 2d (2-3 miles off-route)	Corbridge		✓	✓	✓	✓	train, bus
2d/2e	Wall		✓		✓		
Stage 2d (2-3 miles off-route)	Acomb		✓		✓		
Stage 2d (4.5 miles off-route)	Hexham		✓		✓	✓	train, bus

Stage	Place	Dormitory Beds	Private Rooms	Camping	Meals/Drinks	Food Shop	Transport
2e/3a	Chollerford		✓	✓	✓		✓
3a/3b	Green Carts Farm	✓	✓	✓	Takeaway can be ordered		
3b/3c	Carraw B&B		✓		✓		
3c/3d	Grindon exit		✓		✓		
3d/3e	Housesteads		✓				
3e/4a (off-route)	Once Brewed	✓	✓	✓	✓		✓
4a/4b	Cawfields Quarry	✓	✓	✓	✓	✓	
Stage 4a/4b (3 miles off-route)	Haltwhistle		✓		✓	✓	✓
4b/4c	Holmhead	✓	✓	✓	✓		
Stage 4c (0.4 miles off-route)	Greenhead	✓	✓	✓	✓		
4c/4d	Gilsland		✓		✓		✓
4d/4e	Banks			✓			✓
4e/5a (off-route)	Lanercost Priory		✓		✓		✓

Stage	Place	Dormitory Beds	Private Rooms	Camping	Meals/Drinks	Food Shop	Transport
5a/5b	Walton	✓	✓	✓	✓		🚌
5b/5c	Newtown		✓			🛒	🚌 🚆
Stage 5b/5c (2.5 miles off-route)	Brampton				✓		🚌 🚆
5c/5d	Bleatarn Farm			✓			
5d/5e	Crosby/Low Crosby	✓		✓	✓		🚌 🚆
5e/6a	Carlisle	✓	✓		✓	🛒	🚌
6a/6b	Beaumont		✓	✓			
6b/6c	Boustead Hill	✓		✓			
6c/6d	Glasson		✓		✓		🚌
6d/6e	Port Carlisle		✓		✓		🚌
6e	Bowness-on-Solway	✓	✓		✓		🚌

Food

For most trekkers, breakfast will be provided as part of the overnight package at B&Bs, pubs or hotels: normally a 'Full English' breakfast which is a large helping of bacon, sausage, eggs, mushrooms and black pudding.

For lunch, most accommodation providers will prepare a packed lunch for you: be sure to request this the night before. Alternatively, you could stop for lunch at a pub or café along the route. If your accommodation does not offer evening meals then the staff will usually be able to recommend a pub or restaurant within walking distance.

Most villages have a pub/inn, serving food and excellent beer. In fact, for many trekkers the 'pub grub' and real ale are highlights of the HWP: in recent years, traditional English beer has been enjoying a major revival spurred on by the craft beer revolution.

There are few grocery shops along the HWP so buying self-catering supplies is not a realistic option unless you go to the effort of travelling out to towns and villages away from the trail. There are occasionally unmanned refreshment stalls along the route where you can buy drinks, crisps and chocolate bars but these cannot be relied upon absolutely: they operate on an honesty basis and you place the amount that you owe in a box.

Campers who intend to cook for themselves will largely have to rely on food bought in Newcastle or Carlisle or carried from home (unless they are prepared to travel away from the HWP to re-supply). However, food is heavy so unless you are travelling very quickly, you may not be able to start the trek with all the food that you will require for the full distance. It is much better to accept at the outset that you can only carry a few days' food than to exhaust yourself in the early stages of the trek by carrying too much. Many campers carry a small amount of food which they supplement with meals at pubs and cafés along the way. If you are planning to carry some meals, stick to dried food: water is food's heaviest component. Freeze-dried meals for backpackers are excellent because they are light and are prepared simply by adding boiling water.

Getting to/from Newcastle & Carlisle

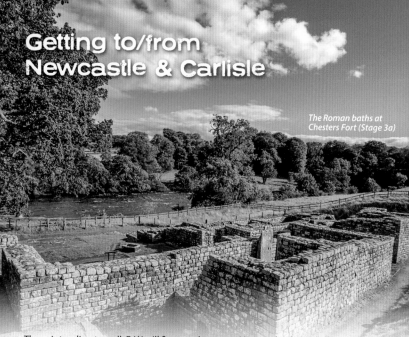

The Roman baths at Chesters Fort (Stage 3a)

Those intending to walk E-W will first need to get to Newcastle. Those walking W-E will first need to get to Carlisle, before onward travel to Bowness-on-Solway.

By air: there are numerous airports in the UK and, in normal times, there are plenty of domestic and international flights available. At the date of press, however, many services were not operating due to COVID-19 and it was not clear if, or when, they would resume. Newcastle itself has an international airport which is only a short ride to the city centre by bus, metro or taxi. You can also travel by metro from Newcastle airport to Wallsend, the start/finish point of the HWP: you have to change trains at Monument.

There is also a small airport near Carlisle which previously had domestic flights but, at the date of press, it was closed and it was unclear if, or when, it would re-open. Glasgow, Edinburgh, Leeds-Bradford, Manchester, Liverpool, Birmingham and London all have airports too. There are trains from each of these cities (and sometimes the airports themselves) to Newcastle and Carlisle.

By train: both Newcastle and Carlisle are well-connected to the rest of GB by rail. To check train times and buy tickets, see www.thetrainline.com.

By bus: there are a variety of buses to Newcastle and Carlisle from other towns and cities. Service providers include National Express (www.nationalexpress.com) and megabus.com. Long-distance buses within the UK often take longer than trains.

By ferry: there are numerous ferries to GB from the island of Ireland and mainland Europe. The most useful service is Amsterdam-Newcastle (www.dfds.com). There are also services from Northern Ireland to Cairnryan in Scotland which is a 2.5-hour drive from Carlisle (www.stenaline.co.uk; www.poferries.com).

By car: you could park your car in Newcastle or Carlisle and use public transport to return to it at the end of the trek (see 'Public Transport along Hadrian's Wall'). You can book reasonably priced parking at www.yourparkingspace.co.uk. Bowness-on-Solway is a small village so safe, considerate and legal parking is difficult to find.

Travel to/from Trail-heads

Primary trail-heads

The River Irthing at Willowford (Stage 4d)

Wallsend: the E trail-head is a stop on Newcastle's metro line: there are frequent trains to/from Newcastle city centre and Newcastle airport (change at Monument). There are also frequent buses from Newcastle city centre to Wallsend (including Stagecoach No.22 & 40 and Go North East 1A/1B and Q3) but few HWP trekkers use them because the metro is so regular and easy to navigate. If you are spending the night in Newcastle, then it might be more convenient to get a taxi from your accommodation directly to Wallsend. For further information on Newcastle transport, see www.nexus.org.uk.

Bowness-on-Solway: the W trail-head is 45min by bus from Carlisle. Stagecoach bus No.93 travels the route, three times in each direction, every Monday to Saturday, excluding public holidays (www.stagecoachbus.com). At the date of press, bus times were as follows:

- ▶ Carlisle to Bowness-on-Solway: 12:40, 16:30 and 18:10
- ▶ Bowness-on-Solway to Carlisle: 07:34, 10:32 and 18:58

Because the bus does not run on Sundays or public holidays, Carlisle Taxi Hire (see below) operates a taxi-bus service on those days between Carlisle and Bowness-on-Solway (£7; advance booking recommended). At the date of press, the times were as follows:

- ▶ Carlisle to Bowness-on-Solway: 09:40 and 16:05
- ▶ Bowness-on-Solway to Carlisle: 10:40 and 17:00

Many E-W trekkers use these services at the end of the trek to get back to Carlisle where they arrange onward travel. W-E trekkers can also use them to get to the start. However, as bus times are irregular, many prefer to arrange a taxi (£25-35) to/from Bowness-on-Solway.

Carlisle taxi operators:

- ▶ Carlisle Taxi Hire (www.carlisletaxihire.co.uk; 01228 424 242)
- ▶ Carlisle Taxis (www.carlisle-taxis.com; 01228 247 365)
- ▶ Carlisle Taxi Company (01228 812 612)
- ▶ Radio Taxis (www.radiotaxis.org.uk; 01228 527 575/515 818)
- ▶ AAA Taxis (www.aaa-taxis.com; 01228 808 777)
- ▶ Executive Cabs (www.executivecabsltd.co.uk; 01228 529 957)
- ▶ Barry's Taxi (www.carlisletaxi.co.uk; 07766 700 020)
- ▶ KV Cars (01228 263 646)

Secondary trail-heads

There are many other escape/access points along the HWP, enabling a walker to join or leave the route: you could use these points to skip sections. The key escape/access points are listed below. For more detail on the transport options, see 'Public Transport along Hadrian's Wall'.

Place	Transport Options
Lemington (Stage 1b)	▶ Stagecoach bus 22 to/from Newcastle ▶ Arriva/Stagecoach bus 685 to/from Newcastle, Heddon-on-the-Wall (Stage 1c/2a), Hexham, Corbridge, Haltwhistle, Brampton and Carlisle (Stage 5e/6a)
Newburn (Stage 1b/1c)	▶ Stagecoach buses 22 and 71 to/from Newcastle
Heddon-on-the-Wall (Stage 1c/2a)	▶ Arriva/Stagecoach bus 685 to/from Newcastle, Hexham, Corbridge, Haltwhistle, Brampton and Carlisle (Stage 5e/6a) ▶ Go North East X84/X85 to/from Newcastle, Corbridge and Hexham
Corbridge (2-3 miles off Stage 2d)	▶ Arriva/Stagecoach bus 685 to/from Newcastle, Heddon-on-the-Wall (Stage 1c/2a), Hexham, Haltwhistle, Brampton and Carlisle (Stage 5e/6a) ▶ Go North East X84/X85 to/from Newcastle, Heddon-on-the-Wall (Stage 1c/2a) and Hexham ▶ Trains to/from Newcastle, Hexham, Haltwhistle, Brampton and Carlisle
Hexham (4.5 miles off Stage 2d)	▶ Arriva/Stagecoach bus 685 to/from Newcastle, Heddon-on-the-Wall (Stage 1c/2a), Corbridge, Haltwhistle, Brampton and Carlisle (Stage 5e/6a) ▶ Go North East X84/X85 to/from Newcastle, Heddon-on-the-Wall (Stage 1c/2a) and Corbridge ▶ Trains to/from Newcastle, Corbridge, Haltwhistle, Brampton and Carlisle
Chesters Fort near Chollerford (Stage 3a)	▶ AD122 bus to/from Brocolitia Fort (Stage 3b), Housesteads Fort (Stage 3d/3e), Once Brewed (Stage 3e/4a), Walltown Quarry (Stage 4b), Haltwhistle and Hexham
Brocolitia Fort (Stage 3b)	▶ AD122 bus to/from Chesters Fort (Stage 3a), Housesteads Fort (Stage 3d/3e), Once Brewed (Stage 3e/4a), Walltown Quarry (Stage 4b), Haltwhistle and Hexham
Housesteads Fort (Stage 3d/3e)	▶ AD122 bus to/from Once Brewed (Stage 3e/4a), Walltown Quarry (Stage 4b), Haltwhistle, Brocolitia Fort (Stage 3b), Chesters Fort near Chollerford (Stage 3a) and Hexham
Once Brewed (Stage 3e/4a)	▶ AD122 bus to/from Walltown Quarry (Stage 4b), Haltwhistle, Housesteads Fort (Stage 3d/3e), Brocolitia Fort (Stage 3b), Chesters Fort near Chollerford (Stage 3a) and Hexham

Place	Transport Options
Walltown Quarry (Stage 4b)	▶ AD122 bus to/from Haltwhistle, Once Brewed (Stage 3e/4a), Housesteads Fort (Stage 3d/3e), Brocolitia Fort (Stage 3b), Chesters Fort near Chollerford (Stage 3a) and Hexham ▶ Go North East bus 185 to/from Haltwhistle, Gilsland (Stage 4c/4d) and Birdoswald Fort (Stage 4d)
Haltwhistle (3 miles from Cawfields Quarry on Stage 4a/4b)	▶ Arriva/Stagecoach bus 685 to/from Newcastle, Heddon-on-the-Wall (Stage 1c/2a), Hexham, Corbridge, Brampton and Carlisle (Stage 5e/6a) ▶ Trains to/from Newcastle, Corbridge, Hexham, Brampton and Carlisle ▶ Go North East bus 185 to/from Walltown Quarry (Stage 4b), Gilsland (Stage 4c/4d) and Birdoswald Fort (Stage 4d)
Gilsland (Stage 4c/4d)	▶ Go North East bus 185 to/from Walltown Quarry (Stage 4b), Haltwhistle, and Birdoswald Fort (Stage 4d) ▶ Border Rambler BR3 to/from Birdoswald Fort (Stage 4d), Banks (Stage 4d/4e), Lanercost Priory (off-route from Stage 4e/5a), Brampton and Newtown (Stage 5b/5c)
Birdoswald Fort (Stage 4d)	▶ Go North East bus 185 to/from Gilsland (Stage 4c/4d), Walltown Quarry (Stage 4b) and Haltwhistle ▶ Border Rambler BR3 to/from Gilsland (Stage 4c/4d), Banks (Stage 4d/4e), Lanercost Priory (off-route from Stage 4e/5a), Brampton and Newtown (Stage 5b/5c)
Banks (Stage 4d/4e)	▶ Border Rambler BR3 to/from Birdoswald Fort (Stage 4d), Gilsland (Stage 4c/4d), Lanercost Priory (off-route from Stage 4e/5a), Brampton and Newtown (Stage 5b/5c)
Lanercost Priory (off-route from Stage 4e/5a)	▶ Border Rambler BR3 to/from Banks (Stage 4d/4e), Birdoswald Fort (Stage 4d), Gilsland (Stage 4c/4d), Brampton and Newtown (Stage 5b/5c)
Newtown (Stage 5b/5c)	▶ Border Rambler BR3 to/from Lanercost Priory (off-route from Stage 4e/5a), Banks (Stage 4d/4e), Birdoswald Fort (Stage 4d), Gilsland (Stage 4c/4d) and Brampton ▶ Border Rambler BR1 to/from Brampton, Crosby-on-Eden (Stage 5e) and Carlisle (Stage 5e/6a). ▶ Border Rambler BR2 to/from Carlisle (Stage 5e/6a)
Brampton (2.5 miles off Stage 5b/5c)	▶ Arriva/Stagecoach bus 685 to/from Newcastle, Heddon-on-the-Wall (Stage 1c/2a), Corbridge, Hexham, Haltwhistle and Carlisle (Stage 5e/6a) ▶ Trains to/from Newcastle, Corbridge, Hexham, Haltwhistle and Carlisle
Oldwall (Stage 5c)	▶ Border Rambler BR3 to/from Lanercost Priory (off-route from Stage 4e/5a), Banks (Stage 4d/4e), Birdoswald Fort (Stage 4d), Gilsland (Stage 4c/4d) and Brampton. ▶ Border Rambler BR1 to/from Brampton, Crosby-on-Eden (Stage 5e) and Carlisle (Stage 5e/6a). ▶ Border Rambler BR2 to/from Carlisle (Stage 5e/6a)

Place	Transport Options
Crosby-on-Eden (Stage 5e)	► Border Rambler BR1 to/from Carlisle (Stage 5e/6a), Brampton and Newtown (Stage 5b/5c)
Carlisle (Stage 5e/6a)	► Arriva/Stagecoach bus 685 to/from Newcastle, Heddon-on-the-Wall (Stage 1c/2a), Hexham, Corbridge, Haltwhistle and Brampton ► Border Rambler BR1 to/from Crosby-on-Eden (Stage 5e), Brampton and Newtown (Stage 5b/5c) ► Border Rambler BR2 to/from Newtown (Stage 5b/5c). ► Trains to/from Newcastle, Corbridge, Hexham, Haltwhistle and Brampton
Drovers Rest Inn near Beaumont (Stage 6a/6b)	► Stagecoach bus 93 to/from Carlisle, Burgh-by-Sands (Stage 6b), Glasson (Stage 6c/6d), Port Carlisle (Stage 6d/6e) and Bowness-on-Solway (Stage 6e)
Burgh-by-Sands (Stage 6b)	► Stagecoach bus 93 to/from Drovers Rest Inn near Beaumont (Stage 6a/6b), Carlisle, Glasson (Stage 6c/6d), Port Carlisle (Stage 6d/6e) and Bowness-on-Solway (Stage 6e)
Glasson (Stage 6c/6d)	► Stagecoach bus 93 to/from Burgh-by-Sands (Stage 6b), Drovers Rest Inn near Beaumont (Stage 6a/6b), Carlisle, Port Carlisle (Stage 6d/6e) and Bowness-on-Solway (Stage 6e)
Port Carlisle (Stage 6d/6e)	► Stagecoach bus 93 to/from Glasson (Stage 6c/6d), Burgh-by-Sands (Stage 6b), Drovers Rest Inn near Beaumont (Stage 6a/6b), Carlisle and Bowness-on-Solway (Stage 6e)

The N gate of Milecastle 37 (Stage 3e)

Walltown Crags (Stage 4b)

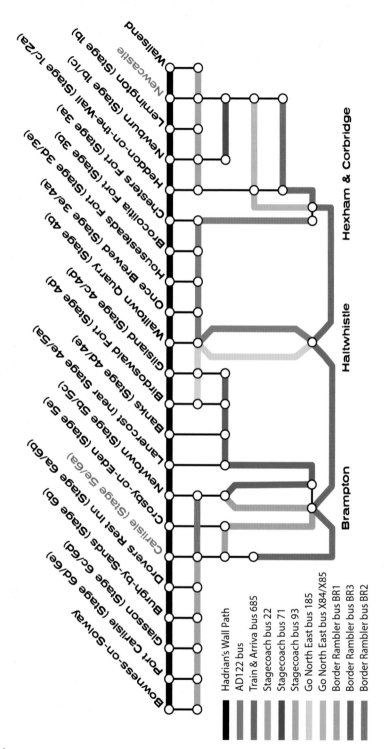

Wallsend
Newcastle
Lemington (Stage 1b)
Newburn (Stage 1b/1c)
Heddon-on-the-Wall (Stage 1c/2a)
Chesters Fort (Stage 3a)
Brocolitia Fort (Stage 3b)
Housesteads Fort (Stage 3d/3e)
Once Brewed (Stage 3e/4a)
Walltown Quarry (Stage 4b)
Gilsland Fort (Stage 4c/4d)
Birdoswald Fort (Stage 4d)
Banks (Stage 4d/4e)
Lanercost (near Stage 4e/5a)
Newtown (Stage 5e)
Crosby-on-Eden (Stage 5b/5c)
Carlisle (Stage 5e/6a)
Drovers Rest Inn (Stage 6a)
Burgh-by-Sands (Stage 6b)
Glasson (Stage 6c/6d)
Port Carlisle (Stage 6d)
Bowness-on-Solway (Stage 6d/6e)

Hexham & Corbridge
Haltwhistle
Brampton

Hadrian's Wall Path
AD122 bus
Train & Arriva bus 685
Stagecoach bus 22
Stagecoach bus 71
Stagecoach bus 93
Go North East bus 185
Go North East bus X84/X85
Border Rambler bus BR1
Border Rambler bus BR3
Border Rambler bus BR2

44

Public Transport along Hadrian's Wall

The many colours of lichen on HW

By train: Northern Rail operates daily trains between Carlisle and Newcastle. They run frequently throughout the day via Brampton, Haltwhistle, Hexham and Corbridge. It is a useful service for trekkers wishing to return to Newcastle/Carlisle at the end of the trek. For times and tickets, see www.northernrailway.co.uk or www.thetrainline.com.

By bus: the key services operating along HW are as follows:

Bus Service	Key Information
Arriva/Stagecoach 685/X85	Daily buses between Carlisle and Newcastle via Heddon-on-the-Wall (Stage 1c/2a), Brampton, Haltwhistle, Hexham and Corbridge. A useful service for trekkers wishing to return to Newcastle/Carlisle at the end of the trek. For times and tickets see www.nexus.org.uk
Go North East AD122 Hadrian's Wall Country Bus	A hop on/hop off tourist bus which operates between April and October along the popular central sections of HW. It runs hourly throughout the day between Hexham and Haltwhistle, via many of HW's most important sites including Chesters Fort (Stage 3a), Housesteads Fort (Stage 3d/3e), Once Brewed (Stage 3e/4a), Vindolanda Fort and Walltown Quarry (Stage 4b). A daily ticket costs £12.50 and gives you 10% discount at most of the forts and museums. For further information, see hadrianswallcountry.co.uk or www.gonortheast.co.uk
Go North East X84/X85	Buses between Newcastle and Hexham via Heddon-on-the-Wall (Stage 1c/2a), Corbridge and Wylam. Operates Monday to Saturday
Go North East 185	Buses between Haltwhistle and Birdoswald Fort (Stage 4d) via Gilsland (Stage 4c/4d) and Walltown Quarry (Stage 4b). Operates Monday to Saturday
Border Rambler BR1	Buses between Carlisle and Newtown (Stage 5b/5c) via Brampton and Crosby-on-Eden (Stage 5e). Operates Tuesday and Friday
Border Rambler BR2	Buses between Carlisle and Newtown (Stage 5b/5c). Operates Thursday
Border Rambler BR3	Buses between Newtown (Stage 5b/5c) and Brampton via Lanercost Priory (off-route from Stage 4e/5a), Banks (Stage 4d/4e), Birdoswald Fort (Stage 4d) and Gilsland (Stage 4c/4d). Operates Wednesday

Bus Service	Key Information
Stagecoach bus 22	Regular buses between Newcastle and Newburn via Lemington. Useful if you wish to skip the section between Wallsend and Newburn. Sometimes it does not operate on Sundays
Stagecoach bus 71	Regular daily buses between Newcastle and Newburn. Useful if you wish to skip the section between Wallsend and Newburn. Sometimes it does not operate on Sundays
Stagecoach bus 93	Buses between Carlisle and Bowness-on-Solway via Port Carlisle (Stage 6d/6e), Glasson (Stage 6c/6d), Burgh-by-Sands (Stage 6b) and Drovers Rest Inn near Beaumont (Stage 6a/6b). Operates Monday to Saturday. See 'Travel to/from Trail-heads'

Further information about bus travel:

Arriva: www.arrivabus.co.uk

Stagecoach: www.stagecoachbus.com

Go North East: www.gonortheast.co.uk

Border Rambler: www.borderramblerbus.co.uk

By taxi

There are countless taxi businesses operating from towns and villages close to HW. They can pick you up from the HWP, drive you to nearby accommodation and leave you back to the HWP the next morning. Some of them operate surprisingly far from their hubs. There are too many taxi businesses to list here but some of the useful services include:

▶ **LA Taxis (Newcastle)**: this reliable business operates along the Newcastle end of HW. They can take you between Heddon-on-the-Wall and Wylam as well as to Newcastle from a variety of places (www.lataxis.co.uk; 0191 287 7777)

▶ **Noda Taxis (Newcastle)**: www.noda-taxis.co.uk; 0191 222 1888

▶ **Blueline Taxis (Newcastle)**: www.bluelinetaxis.com; 0191 262 6666

▶ **Dean Taxis (Newcastle)**: www.deantaxis.co.uk; 0191 444 4444

▶ **Executive Taxis (Corbridge)**: www.executive-taxis.co.uk; 01434 605 601

▶ **Advanced Taxis (Hexham)**: www.advancedtaxis.com; 01434 606 565

▶ **Ecocabs (Hexham)**: www.600600.co.uk; 01434 600 600

▶ **Budget Taxis (Hexham)**: www.budgettaxis.co; 01434 606 332

▶ **Diamond Private Hire (Haltwhistle)**: www.diamond-private-hire.co.uk; 07597 641 222

▶ **Turnbull Taxis (Haltwhistle)**: 01434 320 105

▶ **Brampton Cars (Brampton)**: 01697 73386

▶ **Davison's (Brampton)**: 07402 018 151

▶ **Carlisle taxi services**: see 'Travel to/from Trail-heads'

On the Trail

Costs & budgeting

As vacations go, long-distance trekking in the UK is relatively inexpensive. The walking itself is free as no permits are required. The main components of daily expenditure are food and accommodation/camping: approximate costs are set out below.

	Approximate Cost (subject to change)
Room in pub/inn	£35-50 per person sharing a double/twin room
B&B	£35-50 per person sharing a double/twin room
Bed in hostel	£20-30 per person
Bed in bunkhouse/ camping barn	£10-20 per person
Camping	£7-10 per person
Meal in pub/inn	£12-20
Packed lunch	£6-10
Beer (1 pint)	£3-5

Weather

Northern England has famously green countryside and this beautiful greenery requires plenty of water. The water is of course supplied by rain and GB's location near the Atlantic Ocean ensures that there is plenty of it: the island bears the brunt of many Atlantic fronts as they make their way eastwards. That is not to say that it rains all the time but you should prepare for it, even in summer.

HW country can also be windy and you should take care on the higher and more exposed parts of the HWP. When the sun does shine, there is little shade on the higher sections of the trail.

The HWP runs coast to coast across England and, at any given time, the weather on one part of the trail can be completely different from the weather on another section: for example, it could be raining in Carlisle and sunny in Newcastle or vice versa.

Always get a weather forecast before setting out. Many internet sites provide forecasts, with a varying degree of reliability. The UK Met Office (www.metoffice.gov.uk) is one of the most reliable as it provides regularly updated localised forecasts for different places along the HWP. It also provides, free of charge, an excellent smart-phone app that gives local forecasts.

Maps

In this book, we have included real maps for the entire HWP. Each stage has a 1:25,000 scale map produced by Ordnance Survey, GB's mapping agency. We believe that these are the finest, and most detailed, maps available. They are perfect for navigating the HWP. However, if you would also like sheet maps, there are a number of options:

▶ **OS Explorer 1:25,000**: this is the same mapping that is printed in this book. Four sheets are required to cover the entire HWP: sheets 316 (Newcastle upon Tyne), OL43 (Hadrian's Wall), 315 (Carlisle) and 314 (Solway Firth)

▶ **OS Landranger 1:50,000**: four sheets are required to cover the entire HWP: 88 (Newcastle upon Tyne), 87 (Hexham & Haltwhistle), 86 (Haltwhistle & Brampton) and 85 (Carlisle & Solway Firth)

▶ **Harveys Hadrian's Wall XT40**: this single sheet 1:40,000 waterproof strip map covers the entire trek

However, perhaps the best overall solution is to combine the real maps provided in this book with OS's excellent smart-phone app: it provides 1:25,000 maps for the whole of GB and uses GPS to show your location and direction on the map. As the app's maps are the same as those provided in this book, they can be used together seamlessly. In the past, people often uploaded a series of GPS waypoints to their devices. However, because the OS app is so effective (showing both the HWP route and your actual location), there is now little point in bothering with GPS waypoint uploads. One month's subscription to the app is only £3.99 so it is ideal for HWP walkers.

Paths and waymarking

The HWP normally follows clear paths and tracks. Often, the paths are grassy but some parts are muddy after rain. Much of the countryside is farmland so there are numerous stiles and kissing gates along the route: these allow humans, but not livestock, to pass through. A 'kissing gate' is normally a wooden V-shaped semi-enclosure with the free end of a swinging gate trapped between its arms: it allows just enough room for you to squeeze through.

There are also some short sections along minor roads and the HWP frequently crosses roads and farm tracks: be sure to take care at crossings, looking both ways for traffic. Some years ago, a walker was killed by a passing vehicle near Robin Hood Inn (Stage 2b/2c).

Like many routes in rural England, the HWP has plenty of twists and turns as it negotiates rights-of-way through farmland and villages. Consequently, the route has been extremely well marked and navigation is usually straightforward: almost every junction has a sign or a white acorn (which is the generic symbol for England's National Trails). You will quickly get into a rhythm, looking for the next waymark every time you pass one. In the route descriptions, we do not highlight every junction because the waymarking is so good: generally, we only mention junctions if they are particularly significant or if there are no waymarks. Bear in mind though that waymarking is at the mercy of the environment: for example, signs and waymarks are occasionally obscured by vegetation or destroyed by falling trees.

There are few long climbs or descents on the HWP. Furthermore, gradients are rarely very steep, except for a few short sections in the central part of the trail.

Water

Drinking water will be one of your primary considerations each day. Even in Northern England, the sun can be hot: dehydration and sunstroke are always possibilities. Finding water while on the trail can be tricky. You pass relatively few lakes and rivers and anyway, drinking from them is not advisable: farmers in rural England often use pesticides and fertilisers and traces of these may find their way into the watercourses.

A typical waymark

On rare occasions, taps are provided for walkers in villages. More reliable though are pubs and cafés: most will be happy to fill your water bottles for free if you buy some food or a drink. In fact, licensed premises (those that are authorised to serve alcohol) in England are required by law to provide "free potable water" to their customers upon request. Campsites will also have water taps: if you ask nicely when passing, they may allow you to fill up.

In the introduction to each stage, we list the places where refreshments are available, as well as any water taps, along the route. It is good practice to fill up in the morning at your accommodation, starting the day with at least 1.5 litres. However, water is heavy so you will not want to carry more than you need: plan carefully so that you know where your next fill-up point will be. Furthermore, always check your water levels when you pass a fill-up point.

Storing bags

Often walkers from the UK travel to HW carrying only the gear that they will actually take on the trek. However, trekkers from further afield, and those who want to spend some time elsewhere after the trek, will probably have additional baggage which they need to store while trekking. Normally, a hotel that you have stayed at near the start of the trek will let you store bags until your return: check when booking. At the end of the trek, it is straightforward to get back to the start by train or bus: see 'Public Transport along Hadrian's Wall'. As an alternative, consider a baggage transfer service which delivers your bags to your accommodation each night: see below.

Baggage transfer

A number of businesses offer baggage transfer services along the HWP. They can transfer your bags to your accommodation each night so that you only need to carry a small day-pack on the trail. This spares you from the burden of having to carry a heavy backpack and enables you to pack more clean clothes and some luxuries. The cost is around £7-10/day for a 20kg bag. The available services include:

▶ **Sherpa Van**: www.sherpavan.com; info@sherpavan.com; 01748 826 917

▶ **Hadrian's Bags**: www.hadriansbags.co.uk; info@hadriansbags.co.uk; 01434 634 448/07976 356 459

▶ **Hadrian's Haul**: www.hadrianshaul.com; info@hadrianshaul.com; 07967 564 823

- ▶ **Baggage Transfer Plus**: www.baggagetransferplus.com; 07545 086 857
- ▶ **Brigantes**: www.brigantesenglishwalks.com; info@bagmovers.com; 01756 770 402

Fuel for camping stoves

Airlines will not permit you to transport fuel so campers who are flying to the UK will need to source it upon arrival, before setting out on the trek. There are outdoor shops in Newcastle and Carlisle: methylated spirits and standard screw-in gas canisters are normally available but it is wise to call in advance to check.

- ▶ **Newcastle**: LD Mountain Centre (0191 232 3561);
  Cotswold Outdoor (0191 221 2709); Wildtrak (0191 261 4191)
- ▶ **Carlisle**: Millets (01228 588 253)

If you need petrol or diesel for a multi-fuel stove, there are service stations in Newcastle, Heddon-on-the-Wall and Carlisle.

HWP Passport Scheme

You can purchase a souvenir passport for the HWP: inside there are spaces for seven stamps and along the trail, there are seven stamping stations. You stamp the passport each time you pass a stamping station: if you collect all seven then you are entitled to buy an exclusive enamel badge and certificate. Proceeds from the sale of the passports, badges and certificates are used for the maintenance of the HWP: you can buy them at Segedunum Fort in Wallsend and the King's Arms Pub in Bowness-on-Solway. Passports are also available from Wallsend Guest House & Tea Room (in Bowness-on-Solway), Walltown Quarry Country Park (Stage 4b), Carlisle Tourist Information Centre and online at www.trailgiftshop.co.uk.

A stamping station

The locations of the stamping stations are:

- ▶ **Segedunum Roman Fort (Stage 1a)**: on the outside wall beside the Station Road entrance and in the museum reception
- ▶ **Robin Hood Inn (Stage 2b/2c)**: on the outside wall next to the entrance
- ▶ **Chesters Fort (Stage 3a)**: on the wall beside the car park entrance and in the museum reception
- ▶ **Housesteads Fort (Stage 3d/3e)**: outside the museum entrance
- ▶ **Birdoswald Fort (Stage 4d)**: on an outside wall at the museum entrance and in the museum reception
- ▶ **The Sands Centre, Carlisle (Stage 5e/6a)**: in the café (only available during opening hours)
- ▶ **Bowness-on-Solway (Stage 6e)**: in the Banks Promenade shelter (at the official finish of the HWP), the King's Arms Pub and Lindow Village Hall (beside the King's Arms)

Helping to protect HW

It is truly remarkable that visitors are permitted to walk directly alongside, and touch, one of the finest Roman archaeological sites in the world. For much of the distance of the HWP, you follow in the footsteps of countless Roman soldiers even though the unexcavated remains of the Romans' time in Britain still lie below your feet. This is a privilege which should not be taken for granted. Each and every walker or trekker who sets foot on the HWP has a duty to help to protect the Wall and its surrounds. In addition to the normal rules for walking in the countryside, there are some specific guidelines that you should follow:

► Do not walk on HW or any other ruins

► Do not walk in single file: normally, in the countryside we are taught to walk in single file to prevent new paths from forming. However, on the HWP, preservation of the archaeology overrides the normal requirement to protect the natural environment. Accordingly, you will frequently pass signs requesting that you do not walk on the most obvious path (see image above). By spreading the footfall over a wider area, there is less likelihood of damage to any underlying Roman remains

► Do not walk the HWP in winter when the ground is wetter and more susceptible to damage

► Do not remove any pieces of HW

► Do not stray from the waymarked paths

English Heritage/National Trust

Whilst it is free to walk alongside HW and its milecastle and turrets, there is a charge for entry to the large excavated forts. With the exception of Vindolanda (which is privately owned), these forts are owned/managed by English Heritage and/or the National Trust, which are both charities.

English Heritage looks after more than 400 historic buildings, monuments and sites including many along, or near, HW: to name a few, Lanercost Priory (off-route from Stage 4e/5a), Corbridge Roman Town, Chester's Roman Fort, Housesteads Roman Fort and Birdoswald Roman Fort. These forts are free for English Heritage members.

The National Trust is Europe's largest conservation charity and it cares for coastline, woodlands, countryside and hundreds of historic buildings, gardens and precious collections. It looks after six miles of the best sections of HW and owns Housesteads Roman Fort which is managed by English Heritage: the fort is free for both National Trust and English Heritage members.

Equipment

Sewingshields
Crags (Stage 3d)

The long-distance trekker has no influence over challenges like weather and terrain but can control the contents of a pack carried on the trail. Some trekkers carry only a light day-pack, paying for a baggage transfer service to transport the bulk of their gear to their nightly accommodation: see 'Baggage transfer'. Many others, however, elect to carry all their own gear and it is fair to say that a lot of those people set off carrying equipment which is unnecessary or simply too heavy: this can result in injury and/or exhaustion, leading to abandonment. If you are intending to carry your own gear, then you should give equipment choice careful consideration: it will be crucial to your enjoyment of the trek and the likelihood of success.

When undertaking any long-distance route, you should be properly equipped for the worst terrain and the worst weather conditions which you could encounter. On the HWP, a key consideration is rain: you might not get any in practice but you should expect it when planning. It is a well-used cliché that in England you can experience four seasons in one day and this is certainly true in HW country. In late spring, summer and early autumn, you should carry clothing to combat cold, heat, sun and rain. Even in England, the sun can be strong and getting cold and wet in the hills is unpleasant and can be dangerous.

However, the dilemma is that you should also consider weight and avoid carrying anything unnecessary. The heavier your pack, the harder the trek will be. A trekker's base weight is the weight of his/her pack, excluding food and water. If you are not carrying your own camping gear and cooking equipment, it is perfectly possible to get by with a base weight of 5-6kg (13lb) or less. If you intend to carry camping equipment then, by investing in some modern lightweight gear, you could start the trek with a base weight of 8-9kg (17lb) or less. Many people are quick to tell you that the lighter the gear, the greater the price but that is not always the case. While it is true that lightweight gear can be expensive, there are also some excellent lightweight products which are great value. Tents, sleeping bags and backpacks are the three heaviest items that you will carry so they offer the biggest opportunities for weight-saving. But do not ignore the smaller items either as the weight can quickly add up. So if you can afford it, it is sensible to invest some money in gear before you go. The lighter your gear, the more you will enjoy the trek and the better your chance of success. Be ruthless as every ounce counts.

Recommended basic kit

Layering of clothing is the key to warmth. Do not wear cotton: it does not dry quickly and gets cold. Modern walking clothes are light so make sure that you have a spare set to change into if you get wet.

Boots/Shoes	Good quality, properly fitting and worn in. For the HWP, trail-running shoes are perfectly adequate but many prefer boots with ankle support. As the ground is often damp, shoes/boots with a waterproof membrane (such as Gore-Tex) are a good idea: otherwise you will frequently have wet feet even if it is not raining.
Socks	2 pairs of good quality, quick-drying walking socks: wash one, wear one. Wash them regularly, helping to avoid blisters. As a luxury, it is nice to have a third pair to wear in the evenings.
Waterproof jacket and trousers	A waterproof and breathable rain jacket is essential although it might never leave your pack. Many also carry waterproof trousers.
Base layers	2 T-shirts and underpants of man-made fabrics or merino wool, which wick moisture away from your body: wash one, wear one. As a luxury, it is nice to have a third set to wear in the evenings.
Fleeces	2 fleeces. Man-made fabrics.
Shorts/ Trousers	2 pairs of shorts or walking trousers. Convertible trousers are practical as you can remove the legs on warm days. One pair of shorts and one pair of trousers is also a good combination in summer.
Warm hat	Always carry a warm hat. Even in summer it can be cold on the crags, especially in the evening and early morning.
Gloves	Early or late season trekkers may wish to bring gloves.
Down jacket	Advisable in spring and autumn when low temperatures are more likely, especially in the evening and early morning.
Camp shoes	It is nice to have shoes to wear in the evenings. Flip-flops or Crocs are a common choice as they are light. However, if you have comfortable hiking boots/shoes then you might consider not bringing camp shoes to save weight.
Waterproof pack liner	Most backpacks are not very waterproof. A liner will keep your gear dry if it rains. Many trekkers use external pack covers but we do not find them to be very useful: they flap in the wind and in heavy rain, water still finds its way into the pack around the straps (so you need an internal liner anyway).
Whistle	For emergencies. Many rucksacks have one incorporated into the sternum strap.

Head-light with spare batteries	You will need a flashlight if you are camping. And it is good practice to carry one for emergencies: it can assist if you get caught out late and enable you to signal to rescuers.
Basic first-aid kit	Including plasters, a bandage, antiseptic wipes and painkillers. Blister plasters, moleskin padding or tape (such as Leukotape) can be useful to prevent or combat blisters.
Map and compass	For maps see above. A GPS unit or a smart-phone app can be a useful addition but they are no substitute for a map and compass: after all, batteries can run out and electronics can fail.
Knife	Such as a Swiss Army knife. You are going to need to cut that cheese!
Sunglasses, sun hat, sunscreen and lip salve	Even in England, the sun can be strong so do not set out without these items.
Walking poles	These transfer weight from your legs onto your arms, keeping you fresher. They also save your knees (particularly on descents) and can reduce the likelihood of falling or twisting an ankle.
Phone and charger	A smart-phone is a very useful tool on a trek. It can be used for emergencies. Furthermore, apps for weather, mapping and hotel booking are invaluable. It can also replace your camera to save weight.
Towel	If you are staying at campsites or bunkhouses, you will need a towel: lightweight trekking towels are a sensible choice.
Toiletries	Campers will need to bring soap/shower gel: a small hotel-size bottle should be enough to last the trek, saving a lot of weight. Toothbrush and toothpaste: an almost empty tube will save weight. For those who shave, shaving oil is a lightweight alternative to a can of foam/gel. Leave that make-up behind!
Ziplock plastic bag	A lightweight way of keeping money, passport and credit cards dry.
Ear plugs	Useful if staying in dormitories: you will thank us if someone snores!
Emergency food	Carry some emergency food over and above your planned daily ration. Energy bars, nuts and dried fruit are all good.
Water	Start each day with at least 1.5 litres of water per person. Hydration packs with tubes facilitate more effective hydration by enabling drinking on the move.

Toilet paper and trowel	Bring a backpacking trowel in case nature calls on the trail: bury toilet waste and carry out used toilet paper. Leave no trace.	
Backpack	The weight of a backpack itself is often overlooked but it can be the single heaviest thing that you will carry. The difference in the weights of various packs can be surprisingly large: get a light one. 35-40 litres should be sufficient if you are not carrying camping gear. If you are carrying camping gear, then 45-60 litres should be adequate. If you need a pack bigger than these then you are most likely carrying too much. Look for well-padded shoulder straps and waist band. Much of the weight of the pack should sit on your hips rather than your shoulders. If your budget extends to it, we highly recommend the packs made by the US manufacturer Zpacks: they are a fraction of the weight of most other packs. The Zpacks Arc Blast is 55 litres yet it weighs just over 500g (20 oz): it is an excellent choice for camping on the HWP.	

Additional gear for campers

Tent: this is one of the heaviest things that you will carry so it provides a big opportunity for weight saving. Some 2-person tents weigh more than 3kg while others weigh less than 0.6kg. The heaviest ones are normally built for extreme winter conditions and are overkill for the HWP. The lightest ones are quite fragile but this is not normally an issue on the HWP where campsites are often grassy. Although a few premium brands charge a lot for their products and there are some very expensive tents at the lightest end of the scale, these days there are plenty of lightweight tents available at a reasonable price. Tents weighing 1 to 1.5kg often strike a good balance between price, longevity and weight. Consider money spent here as an investment in your well-being and enjoyment of one of the world's great trails. Believe us when we say that a few kgs can be the difference between success and failure.

Your tent should be waterproof to ensure that you stay dry during rainy nights. If you are going to use a very light tent then a footprint can be a good idea to protect its base: 'footprint' is a trendy, modern word for what used to be known as a groundsheet. Sometimes you can buy footprints specific to your tent model but we prefer to use a sheet of Tyvek which can be cut to size: Tyvek is extremely tough and is cheaper, and normally lighter, than most branded footprints.

Tent Pegs: tent weights provided by manufacturers normally exclude the weight of the pegs. The pegs actually provided with tents tend to be quite heavy and many trekkers buy replacement ones which are lighter. Six heavy pegs can weigh as much as 240g while 6 light pegs can weigh as little as 6g. There are many different types available these days and it is important to match the peg with the type of ground they will be used in. The ground on the HWP is soft and normally grassy so it is usually easy to get pegs into it. Accordingly, they do not need to be too strong.

Sleeping bag: each bag has a 'comfort rating': This is the lowest temperature at which the standard woman should enjoy a comfortable night's sleep. There is also a 'lower comfort limit' which is for men. That may sound simple but it is not. Although all reputable sleeping bag manufacturers use the same independent standard, the bags are not tested in the same place so there is a lack of consistency amongst ratings. Also, the ratings are designed with an average man and woman in mind but every person is different: some people get colder than others. The ratings should therefore be used as a guide only and it is wise to choose a bag with a comfort rating which is a few degrees lower than the night temperatures that you will encounter. In June, July and August a bag rated between 5 and 10°C is normally sufficient, depending on whether you 'sleep hot' or 'sleep cold'. In early and late season, you may want something warmer. However, you do not want to bring a bag that is much too warm as that would add unnecessary weight to your pack.

Unfortunately, with sleeping bags, price tends to be inversely proportional to weight. This is largely because the lightest bags are filled with goose/duck down which is expensive. Synthetic bags are also available but they are much heavier so down is the better choice for the HWP. The disadvantage of down bags is that they can lose their warmth if they get wet but that is less likely if you have a good tent and pack liner. Our advice is first to decide what comfort rating you will require. Then choose the lightest bag (with that rating) which you can afford.

Sleeping mat: this serves two purposes. Firstly, it makes it comfortable for you to sleep on the hard ground. Secondly, it insulates you from the ground's cold surface. There are three types: air, self-inflating and closed-cell foam. The advantages and disadvantages of each are set out below. For the HWP, weight is normally more of an issue than warmth so we prefer air mats.

Sleeping Mat Type	Pros	Cons
Air mats: need to be blown up	Lightest Very comfortable Most compact when packed Thicker: good for side sleepers	Most expensive Hard work to inflate Can be punctured Less warm than self-inflating
Self-inflating mats: a combination of air and closed-cell foam. The mat partially inflates itself when the valve is opened	Warmest Very comfortable Quite compact More durable than air mats Firmness is adjustable by adding air	Heavier More expensive than closed-cell foam Can be punctured
Closed-cell foam mats	Light Least expensive Most durable Cannot be punctured	Not compact: needs to be strapped to the outside of your pack Least warm Least comfortable

Pillow: some use rolled-up clothing but we prefer inflatable trekking pillows which only weigh around 50g.

Stove: you should choose a stove that uses a type of fuel which is available on the HWP. Airlines do not permit you to carry fuel on planes so, if you are flying to the UK, you will need to source fuel on arrival. Although methylated spirits are sometimes stocked in outdoor shops, these days gas is more widely available (see 'On the Trail'). Most gas stoves are designed to fit generic screw-on canisters (not Campinggaz) which are readily available in the UK. Canisters for Campinggaz stoves (which are popular in France) are much harder to find so are not a good choice for the HWP. Multi-fuel stoves that burn petrol and/or diesel are useful though: there are service stations in Newcastle, Heddon-on-the-Wall and Carlisle.

Hundreds of different stoves are available, some more complicated than others. Often the lightest ones are the most simple and often the most simple ones are relatively inexpensive. If, like most campers, you will eat dried food such as pasta and rice then your stove will need to do little more than boil water. A basic stove which mounts on top of a gas canister will therefore be adequate: such a stove should also be cheap and lightweight (less than 100g).

Pots: if, like most campers, you eat dried food such as pasta and rice then you will only need one pot which will do little more than boil water. To save weight, go for the smallest pot that you can get away with. For example, if you are travelling solo and planning to use freeze-dried backpacking meals then you would need nothing bigger than a 500-600ml pot. Titanium pots are usually the lightest but they are slightly more expensive. Get the lightest one that you can afford.

Fork/Spoon: we love Sporks! They are made of plastic and have a spoon at one end and a fork at the other. They weigh a mere 9g and cost very little

*Housesteads Crags
(Stage 3e)*

Safety

Beautiful farmland on Stage 2d

On a calm summer's day, HW country is paradise. But a sudden weather shift or an injury can change things dramatically so treat the hills and crags with respect and be conscious of your experience levels and physical capabilities. The following is a non-exhaustive list of recommendations:

▶ The fitter you are at the start of your trip, the more you will enjoy the hiking.

▶ Start early to avoid walking during the hottest part of the day and to allow surplus time in case something goes wrong.

▶ Do not stray from the waymarked paths so as to avoid getting lost and to help prevent erosion of the landscape.

▶ Before you set out each day, study the route and make plans based upon the abilities of the weakest member of your party.

▶ Get a weather forecast (daily if possible) and reassess your plans in light of it. Avoid exposed routes if the weather is uncertain.

▶ Never be too proud to turn back if you find the going too tough or if the weather deteriorates.

▶ Bring a map and compass and know how to use them.

▶ Carry surplus food and clothing for emergencies.

▶ Avoid exposed high ground in a thunderstorm. If you get caught out in one then drop your walking poles and stay away from trees, overhanging rocks, metal structures and caves. Generally accepted advice is to squat on your pack and keep as low as possible.

▶ In the event of an accident, move an injured person into a safe place and administer any necessary first-aid. Keep the victim warm. Establish your exact coordinates and, if possible, use your cell-phone to call for help. The emergency number is 999. If you have no signal then send someone for help.

▶ When cooking on a camping stove, place the stove on the ground. Do not use it on a picnic table. We witnessed a walker knocking over his stove and spilling boiling water on his legs: this is a sure-fire way to end your trek.

General Information

Language: English is the main language.

Charging electronic devices: the UK uses a 3-pin plug. Visitors from outside the UK or Ireland will need an adapter. Some campsites, bunkhouses and camping barns facilitate the charging of electronic devices but this may not be possible at the more basic places. Some people carry their own portable charging devices.

Money: the UK uses Sterling (£). There are ATMs in most towns and in many service stations but rarely in smaller villages. On the HWP itself, there are ATMs only in Newcastle, Heddon-on-the-Wall (at the service station) and Carlisle. Credit cards are accepted almost everywhere.

Visas: citizens of the European Union, Australia, New Zealand, Canada or the US do not need a visa for short tourist trips to the UK.

Cell-phones: there is network in most places along the HWP. However, in the more remote parts, it can occasionally be difficult to get a signal. When network is available, it is likely to be a 3G/4G service enabling access to the internet from smart-phones.

International dialling codes: the country code for the UK is +44. If dialling from overseas, the 0 in UK area codes is omitted.

WiFi: nearly all hotels, pubs and B&Bs have WiFi. Some campsites, camping barns and bunkhouses may not offer it. We indicate in the Accommodation Listings exactly which places provide WiFi.

Emergencies and rescue: rescue services are normally charities financed by grants and public donations. Usually their services are free and are provided by unpaid volunteers. The emergency number is 999: ask for 'mountain rescue'.

Insurance: depending upon your nationality, any required medical treatment in the UK may not be provided free of charge so it is wise to purchase travel insurance which covers hiking.

Ticks: as is often the case in Europe, ticks are present in HW country. They can carry Lyme disease or tick-borne encephalitis so check yourself regularly. Remove ticks with tweezers (making sure you get all of it out) and then disinfect the area.

Tourist Information: there are tourist information centres at Newcastle (Stage 1a/1b), The Sill at Once Brewed (Stage 3e/4a), Walltown Quarry (Stage 4b) and Carlisle (Stage 5e/6a). Information is also available online from the following sources:

- ▶ **www.nationaltrail.co.uk:** information on all England's National Trails, including the HWP

- ▶ **www.hadrianswallcountry.co.uk:** official visitor information on HW

- ▶ **www.northumberlandnationalpark.org.uk:** the central sections of the HWP pass through the NNP

- ▶ **www.english-heritage.org.uk:** this charity owns/manages many of the most important sites on HW (see 'English Heritage/National Trust')

- ▶ **www.nationaltrust.org.uk:** this charity own/manages many of the most important parts of HW (see 'English Heritage/National Trust')

- ▶ **www.vindolanda.com:** the Vindolanda Trust owns Vindolanda Fort and Carvoran Roman Army Museum

Wildlife

Much of the fauna in HW country is similar to that in other parts of the UK. There are deer, foxes, badgers, rabbits, grey squirrels, hedgehogs, mice, shrews, voles, stoats, weasels and bats. However, the HWP passes through the NNP which is the least populated National Park in the UK and therefore provides ideal conditions for some more rare species such as otters, hares and red squirrels. Hares and rabbits are often confused but in fact they are quite easy to tell apart: hares have distinctive pointy faces and longer ears (with black tips). It is of interest to the HWP trekker that, as well as building HW, it is thought that the Romans introduced rabbits to Britain! There are snakes too: the adder is poisonous but rarely spotted. On the higher crags, mammals (other than sheep) are few and far between: you are much more likely to spot an animal in the surrounding fields, hedgerows and forests. In the rivers, there are salmon and trout.

Much of the bird life is also similar to that in other parts of the UK. Magpies and crows are ubiquitous as are many of the usual species of small birds. Sparrowhawks, kestrels, peregrine falcons, skylarks, jays, ravens, pheasants and grouse (red and black) are present too. The NNP also has wading birds including lapwing, snipe, oystercatcher and curlew (which is the emblem of the park). The curlews normally spend summers breeding in upland areas and return to the sea in winter. Wading birds are also common on the Solway coast at the W end of the HWP.

Plants and Flowers

HW runs over the tops
of the crags of the NNP

There are a variety of habitats along the HWP including much farmland and woodland. In the central sections, HW crosses the wild heather moorland and high crags of the NNP. In fact, heather moorland (which occurs only in GB) covers 70% of the NNP. It developed over thousands of years, as humans felled woodland to create grazing for livestock. Red Grouse feed on the heather which flowers in August giving the hillsides a vibrant purple hue.

The bluebells in the woodlands are a sight to behold in April/May. Gorse is also widespread and its yellow flowers are a dominating feature of the countryside in spring. Anyone who walks through a section of bright gorse will be struck by the mouth-watering coconut aroma. The NNP also has some of the best hay meadows in Europe which contain a wide variety of wild-flowers including thistles, wood cranesbill and yellow rattle.

Those walking the HWP in late summer and early autumn will find blackberries seemingly everywhere. Purple sloe berries (which grow on blackthorn) are common too: they look like giant blueberries but they do not taste like them! In fact, sloe berries are only really palatable when added to gin.

In woodland, conifers are common as are oak, sycamore, birch, hazel and ash trees. On the wild crags of the HWP, you will spot trees standing alone: often these are hawthorn or rowan trees.

Hadrian's Wall

HW was one of the largest and most important structures built by the Romans (who were renowned masters of engineering). It was 73 miles (80 Roman miles) long and traversed Northern England from coast to coast, between Bowness-on-Solway and Newcastle. It is thought that it was 4 to 5m high. It marked the NW extremity of the immense Roman empire which stretched from Britain all the way to the Middle East and North Africa.

The Wall was commenced in CE122 on the orders of the emperor Hadrian who visited Britain in that year. It probably took between six and ten years to complete. Initially, it was built as a stone wall in the E and a turf wall in the W but plans evolved over time and the turf section was later replaced by a stone wall: it is not clear exactly when. The turf wall originally ran from Bowness-on-Solway to the River Irthing at Willowford but eventually, a stone wall spanned the full 73 miles. The Wall was built largely by the soldiers of the legions (Rome's professional army).

Construction

The stone wall was mostly sandstone or limestone and had a foundation of slabs set in clay. Stone was usually quarried locally. The rectangular stones on the outer faces of the Wall were only faced and finished on the outside: on the inside they were left rough. First a few courses of the facing stones would have been laid with mortar. Then rubble and mortar would have been used to fill the middle cavity (see image above). Afterwards, the next few courses of facing stones would have been laid on top, more rubble placed inside and so on. Drains were laid through the foundations in places where water collected.

The turf wall was made of blocks of turf. So little of it remains that it is difficult to determine exactly how it was constructed. It is thought that the W section of HW was originally built in turf because there was no limestone for mortar in this area.

The stone wall was originally planned to be 10 Roman feet (2.97m) wide. However, before completion, it was decided (at the same time as the decision to build forts on the line of HW (see below)) to reduce the width to 6 to 8 Roman feet (1.78 to 2.37m). Most likely this was done to save time. The **'Broad Wall'** sections were built before the decision to construct forts on the line of the Wall and the **'Narrow Wall'** sections were built afterwards.

Along the HWP, you will frequently notice sections of Narrow Wall constructed on top of the originally planned broader foundations. The decision to build Narrow Wall was taken before the turf wall was rebuilt in stone: accordingly, W of the River Irthing all the stone wall was Narrow Wall with no broad foundations. Interestingly, the standard of masonry is inferior in the last sections of HW to be completed, suggesting that there was a rush to finish the structure.

HW had four bridges across the Rivers Tyne, North Tyne, Irthing and Eden although none of these still exist. Inexplicably, the Wall itself continued across the bridges.

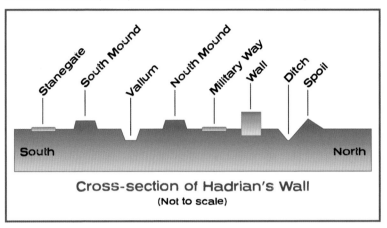

Cross-section of Hadrian's Wall
(Not to scale)

Milecastles

Fortified gatehouses (known as 'milecastles') were built along HW at intervals of 1 Roman mile. They were made of stone or timber and had gates at the front and rear, allowing passage through the Wall. They had two or four rooms inside and a stairway enabling access to a tower (or possibly the top of HW itself). Each milecastle garrisoned between 8 and 32 men so one or two of the rooms would have been barracks to house the soldiers. Modern convention is to number the milecastles in order (regardless of whether they still exist or not), starting in the E with Milecastle 1 and finishing in the W with Milecastle 80.

Milecastle 39
(Stage 3e)

Turrets

Between each milecastle there were two stone observation towers (known as 'turrets'): with true Roman exactness, they were usually spaced precisely ⅓ mile apart. They were 6m square and were recessed into the Wall. The turrets would have had a room with a hearth on the ground floor so that soldiers could keep warm. In the CE180s, many turrets on HW were abandoned probably because the decision to

Turret 45a
(Stage 4b)

build forts on the line of the Wall had made them redundant. Modern convention is to label the turrets by reference to the milecastle immediately to the E of it. For example, between milecastle 38 and 39, there would have been two turrets: the turret immediately to the W of Milecastle 38 is known as Turret 38a and the turret immediately to the E of Milecastle 39 is known as Turret 38b.

The Ditch

The Ditch

Just to the N of HW, a defensive ditch was dug which ran, almost unbroken, from coast to coast. It was V-shaped: 8 to 12m wide and 2.7 to 3m deep. The material dug out of the ditch (the '**spoil**') was normally placed on the N side of it to make the ditch seem deeper.

Forts

The initial scheme for HW did not incorporate forts at the Wall itself: instead there was a system of 'hinterland' forts situated well to the S of it. However, only a few years after commencement of the Wall, this scheme was modified before it was fully implemented: it was decided to build new forts along the Wall itself. The purpose of this change was to facilitate quicker movement of troops, allowing access through HW for larger forces: under the original scheme, soldiers would have had to travel a number of miles from hinterland forts up to HW, where they would have squeezed through the narrow gates of the milecastles.

This was a significant decision as it meant that parts of the Wall already constructed had to be demolished to allow for the construction of 12 or 13 new forts on the line of the Wall itself. It also rendered the milecastles (many of which had already been built) less useful although they were still completed as originally planned. The modifications suggest that greater forces were then required N of the Wall, perhaps to deal with trouble from local tribes.

Vindolanda Roman Fort

The new forts were evenly spaced ($7\frac{1}{3}$ Roman miles apart) except where forts were required at the river crossings. Some hinterland forts were abandoned but several (such as Vindolanda) remained in operation.

The Vallum

Around the same time that it was decided to build forts along the line of HW, plans were drawn up to construct what is now known as the 'Vallum'. It was a complicated scheme of earthworks creating a 37m cleared area to the S of HW which would have been difficult for anyone to cross unobserved. It effectively created a military zone which protected HW from the rear. After it was built, it was only possible to cross the Wall at the forts: crossing points were reduced from 79 to 14. During the

The Vallum (Stage 2c)

peaceful third century, the Vallum went out of use and civilians built between it and the forts.

The Cumbrian Coast

From Bowness-on-Solway, at the W end of HW, the chain of milecastles and towers was continued S for at least 26 miles along the Cumbrian coast. No physical wall was built as the sea itself defined the boundary. Like HW, the 'sea wall' was unlikely to have been a defensive boundary to repel an attack from the sea. Rather it would have controlled traffic across the estuary (the Solway Firth).

Why was Hadrian's Wall built?

Although it did provide military benefits and was patrolled by soldiers, HW was not built primarily for military purposes: it was intended to separate the Romans from the people of the N and to control the movement of people into, and out of, the Roman Empire. The milecastles and turrets facilitated surveillance over the land to the N but HW was not really intended to be a defensive rampart: the initial scheme did not provide for large forts along the Wall and the milecastles and turrets would not have garrisoned enough soldiers to repel a serious attack.

The gates in the milecastles allowing access through HW indicate that the Wall was designed to control movement rather than prevent it. Traders, farmers and other civilians would have been allowed through to sell goods, visit relatives, or move livestock: it is likely that they would have been forced to pay customs duties. The gates would also have allowed the soldiers through to patrol to the N of HW and to maintain the Wall.

Although HW was technically wide enough to allow soldiers to patrol along its top, there is in fact no evidence that they did so. Furthermore, the Wall was probably too narrow to serve as a fighting platform.

Who was Hadrian?

Publius Aelius Hadrianus was born in CE76. His family hailed from Southern Spain and were some of the first citizens from Rome's provinces to enter the Senate. When his father

died, Hadrian became the ward of Trajan (his father's cousin) who was also from Spain. Hadrian was at Trajan's side during many of his successful military campaigns.

He became Emperor in 117 at the age of 41 and reigned during the peak of the Roman Empire's success. He had 30 legions at his command (almost 200,000 professional soldiers). He was probably the most itinerant emperor in Rome's history, visiting all 36 of the provinces in 11 years. He died in 138 at Baia near Naples.

The Romans in Britain

The reconstruction of HW at Vindolanda Roman Fort

Invasion

The Romans first invaded Britain in BCE55, led by Julius Caesar. His campaign started too late in the season and very nearly ended in disaster. However, he returned in BCE54 and, after securing the submission of some of the British tribes, he sailed back to mainland Europe before winter arrived. Almost 100 years passed before Rome set its military sights on Britain once again. The Roman Republic had by then become an empire and Emperor Claudius needed a military victory to bolster his authority, settle revolt and secure his dynasty: Britain seemed like an easy mark. In CE43, an invasion force disembarked on the shores of what is now Kent. Claudius himself arrived in August of that year bringing with him, amongst other things, a number of war-elephants. After a series of battles, 11 British kings submitted to Rome including one from as far away as the Orkney Islands. Claudius returned triumphantly to Rome, his authority secure. The new province of 'Britannia' would remain part of the Roman Empire for almost 400 years.

Expansion & retreat

Claudius eventually lost interest in further expansion of the Empire and things were relatively quiet in Britannia until his successor (Nero) sought to expand the province. In CE60, Nero's brutal regime in Britannia caused a rebellion in the S, led by the famous Queen Boudica. After the uprising was quelled, plans for expansion were once again shelved.

Vespasian, who became emperor in 69, understood Britain, having served there during the invasion by Claudius. He appointed a series of competent governors who conquered significant territory in Northern England and South Wales. By the time of Vespasian's death in 79, the Roman army was approaching the River Tay in what is now Scotland. It is thought that, around this time, Rome built the Gask Ridge (running NE across Perthshire), its first physical frontier in Britain: it was a series of watchtowers placed a mile apart and connected by a road. The frontier ran along a pre-existing boundary separating the Caledonii people from their neighbours, the Venicones.

Emperor Domitian continued the advance in 82 but this was stopped when one of Britannia's legions was withdrawn to deal with trouble on the Danube. Between 86 and 88, the remaining legions withdrew to the line stretching between the Forth and Clyde estuaries.

By 100, the Romans had further withdrawn to the Tyne-Solway line, close to what would eventually become the line of HW: it is thought that Emperor Trajan, one of Rome's most successful emperors, was responsible for this decision. The Romans had previously built a road (known as the '**Stanegate**') between the important forts at Carlisle in the W and Corbridge in the E and during Trajan's reign this broadly marked the frontier. The Romans began to build forts in stone nearby and the following few years were more peaceful.

Trajan is normally thought of as a man with a mission and during his reign, the Roman Empire grew to its largest size. However, as the known world grew and the Romans travelled further from the Mediterranean, the countryside and its people would have seemed more alien. Although he craved military success, perhaps it became clear to Trajan that Rome would not be able to conquer all the world and that it would need boundaries along the Empire's frontiers.

The building of Hadrian's Wall

When Hadrian became emperor in 117, there was trouble in many Roman provinces. The Empire, which had been expanded greatly under Trajan, was looking to be overstretched. In the E of the Empire, Hadrian relinquished territory previously gained by Trajan. He abandoned any thought of future conquest and sought to consolidate, seeking peace within existing frontiers. This was a significant shift in Rome's policy: previously there were no limits to Roman ambition as they sought to conquer all of the known world but now the Empire was to have firm territorial boundaries.

In 117, the Britons were proving difficult to control and the legions sustained heavy casualties: Hadrian sent 3,000 extra troops to Britain. Although control was re-established in 119, Hadrian decided to give Britannia serious personal attention. In 121, soldiers started building a huge fence along the frontier of the Empire in Germany and Hadrian probably had this in mind when he arrived in Britannia in 122 with an entourage of hundreds of people. As he toured the frontier regions, the plan for HW took shape. A wall along the frontier would keep things peaceful by discouraging raiding and attacks and enabling the Romans to monitor the movement of the people. The Stanegate which was already in place would provide the essential line of communication along the Wall. And there was plenty of rock to be quarried along the route, providing the raw materials.

Centurial Stone at Willowford Farm

Although HW was probably conceived in 122, it is possible that building works did not commence until 123. Building began at the E end of the frontier by a workforce provided by three legions (approximately 7,000 men). Later on, other provincial soldiers and sailors from the Roman fleet assisted. It is thought that the Wall took between six and ten years to complete.

The Antonine Wall

When Hadrian died in 138, his adopted son, Antoninus Pius, became emperor. Needing a victory to stamp his authority on the Empire, he quickly decided to expand the province of Britannia, reversing Hadrian's policy of consolidation. In 140, the army advanced N and within two years had extended the frontier by around 90 miles. To consolidate the new territory, the Romans built new roads and forts. In 142 they also began constructing another wall (now known as the 'Antonine Wall') which had the same purpose as HW: it ran for 37 miles across what is now Scotland, between the Clyde in the W and the Firth of Forth in the E. It was half the length of HW and was made from turf rather than stone. It was ⅔ of the width of HW and about the same height. It had a ditch but no structure equivalent to the Vallum.

Once the Antonine Wall was completed, HW was abandoned and left open to traffic. The garrisons may have withdrawn to the older Stanegate forts (Vindolanda, Corbridge and Carlisle). It seems astonishing that such a significant structure (that took up to a decade to complete) could be abandoned so soon but for the Romans this decision would have been easier to make: HW was built by the legions, professional soldiers who had to be paid anyway. Furthermore, the building materials were lying in the ground waiting to be used at no cost.

Re-occupation of Hadrian's Wall

In the 160s, HW was repaired and re-occupied. The rebuilding of the turf sections in stone was completed too. It is thought that the Antonine Wall was abandoned somewhere between 158 and 164. The surviving evidence does not explain why this happened but Britain was never a key priority for Rome and perhaps some of the soldiers stationed there were required elsewhere in the Empire: it may not have been possible to control the territory N of HW with reduced forces. However, this did not mark a complete withdrawal back to HW as some forts N of HW continued to be occupied.

In the early 180s, during the reign of Commodus, there was war in Britain, putting the entire province at risk. Native armies crossed a wall but it is not certain which one. However, damage to HW around this time suggests that it may have been the wall in question. Order was restored by 184 but troubles continued.

The 3rd and 4th centuries

By 208, the unrest had become serious once again and emperor Septimius Severus arrived in Britain and embarked on a campaign into Scotland. His losses were great but the natives eventually capitulated. Not long afterwards, Severus died and the territory was conceded again by his son, Caracalla, who succeeded him. Caracalla may also have initiated repairs to HW, refurbished forts and built new bridges across the North Tyne and the Irthing. Some turrets were abandoned and the double gates in Milecastles were blocked up. Outpost forts N of HW were strengthened to facilitate patrolling and surveillance in those areas. The Wall would have continued to control the movement of people and the number of troops there was

Building Stone at Chesters Roman Fort Museum

INCISED CARVING OF PHALLUS

CSIR407

CHESTERS

B8
CH292

increased but significant forces were also stationed N of it in four outpost forts. These measures discouraged raids and there was peace along HW for most of the remainder of the 3rd century.

By the end of the third century, the size of the army along HW had decreased substantially and the Wall, and some of its forts, had fallen into disrepair. At the start of the 4th century, much needed repairs were carried out along HW, possibly in response to a new threat from Ireland. The century was peaceful until 342 when the Picts (a united federation of local tribes) attacked the outpost forts. The trouble with the Picts continued as the century progressed and in 367, there was a coordinated attack on the province by the Picts, Scots, Saxons and Franks: for two years, they rampaged across the land and many Roman soldiers deserted. It was a huge shock to Rome at a time when the Empire was already declining. Order was restored in 369 and the frontier was strengthened again. However, the peace was short-lived and the Picts continued to cause problems.

The decline of the Roman Empire

In 378, the Roman army was defeated by the Goths at the Battle of Adrianople, in the E of the Empire. The Roman losses were huge and it was a significant blow to Rome. As the 4th century came to a close, internal power struggles weakened the Empire at a time when unrest from native populations was heightened. The Empire was crumbling. In 401, many troops were withdrawn from Britain to deal with trouble in mainland Europe. Political unrest in Rome continued and in 406, the Vandals and others rampaged across the western Empire causing chaos. In 407, Constantine III withdrew more troops from Britain to Europe in an attempt to win the imperial throne. After this, the authority of the Romans in Britain simply slipped away and was never restored. Britons started to manage their own affairs. Many of the remaining soldiers would have drifted away from the HW garrisons when they stopped getting paid, some turning to farming. Others continued to occupy the forts now as civilians. Without the Roman Empire and its soldiers, the Wall served no purpose and was left to decay. Within 50 years, Britain entered what is often referred to as the 'Dark Ages': coins stopped circulating and the manufacture of pottery ceased.

Hadrian's Wall at Black Carts (Stage 3b)

Hadrian's Wall Timeline

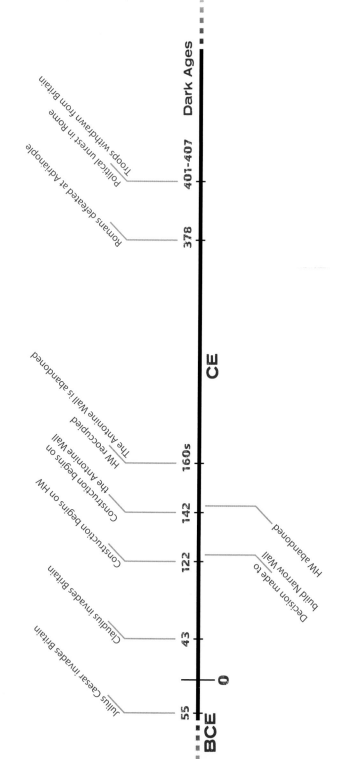

BCE

55 — Julius Caesar invades Britain

0

CE

43 — Claudius invades Britain

122 — Construction begins on HW

Decision made to build Narrow Wall

HW abandoned

142 — Construction begins on the Antonine Wall

160s — HW reoccupied

The Antonine Wall is abandoned

378 — Romans defeated at Adrianople

401-407 — Political unrest in Rome

Troops withdrawn from Britain

Dark Ages

What happened to Hadrian's Wall after the Romans?

Cawfield Crags (Stage 4a)

Relatively little is known about life in HW country in the years following the decline of the Roman Empire. The lack of written materials, coins and pottery means that archaeological evidence is scanty. As time went on, shepherds used the Wall, and its milecastles and turrets, as shelters for summer grazing. These shelters were called 'shields' and many place names along HW still incorporate this word: for example, Sewingshields and Winshield. Elsewhere, the stone of the Wall was just sitting there, already quarried and dressed, crying out to be used for other structures. In particular, the section of the Wall W of Birdoswald was heavily plundered and very little of it remains. The central section along the high crags fared better, largely because of its relative remoteness.

Much of the E sections of HW fell victim to the Jacobite uprising in the 18th century. In 1745, Bonnie Prince Charlie invaded England via Carlisle. The English armies needed a route to get troops, artillery and supplies from Newcastle to Carlisle and so they demolished large parts of HW and built a road on top of it. This road is now the B6318 but is still known as the 'Military Road'.

Preservation of Hadrian's Wall

Walltown Crags were under threat in the early 20th century

After the construction of the Military Road, HW country became more accessible and in 1801, William Hutton walked the full length of the Wall and wrote a book about it. Interest in the Wall grew and in 1840, John Hodgson, curate of Jarrow, was the first to argue that it was built under Hadrian rather than Severus (as previously thought). In 1849, John Collingwood led a tour along HW and later published a book, 'The Roman Wall'. Then in the 1850s, Henry MacLaughlin produced a map of HW country.

John Clayton

It was John Clayton who really started the drive for preservation of HW. Born in 1792, he inherited Chesters estate in 1843. He was the Town Clerk of Newcastle and cleverly invested in building projects during the construction of Georgian Newcastle. He used the profits to buy up land along HW. By the time he died in 1890, he owned five forts and much of the central section of HW that visitors marvel at today.

His workmen excavated many sites and rebuilt large sections of HW from rubble still lying in situ. They built up the outer courses and filled them with rubble and mortar. Then they capped the wall with turf to protect it from the elements. Interestingly, the Romans had used mortar in the outer faces of the Wall but Clayton rebuilt them as dry-stone walls without mortar. His techniques would horrify modern archaeologists but, without his energy and funding, much less of HW would be on show today and perhaps the HWP would not even exist. The structures which he protected include Black Carts Turret 29a (Stage 3a), milecastles at Housesteads Fort (Stage 3d/3e), Cawfields Milecastle 42 (Stage 4a) and Chesters Fort including the bridge abutment (Stage 3a). You can view his staggering collection of Roman relics at the incredible museum at Chesters Fort.

20th century threats

Not everyone cared about the preservation of HW as much as John Clayton. Even in the 1920s, quarrying was still destroying parts of the remaining Wall near Cawfields and Walltown. The Clayton estate protected large sections of HW until 1929, when the estate was broken up. The National Trust then began to acquire substantial portions of the estate's property but they did not own the mineral rights. In the same year, John Wake (who already had an interest in Cawfields Quarry) leased the mineral rights of land which included five of the most spectacular miles of HW (between Cawfields Milecastle 42 and turret 37a near Housesteads Fort). He planned to quarry on the S side of HW to within 10 feet of it. On the N side of the crags, there are large drops so the plans would have left HW literally teetering on a knife edge. Lobbying by celebrities, such as Rudyard Kipling and John Buchan, helped persuade the Government to step in: new legislation was brought in which ensured that the Wall could not be threatened in the same way again.

Ironically, early archaeological excavations also contributed to the loss of some structures. Often archaeologists would systematically clear the ground of stone to locate the original structures built under Hadrian. This enabled them to produce accurate ground plans, however, it meant that much evidence of post-Hadrianic development was lost.

The Birleys

In 1929, Eric Birley, a young scholar who had a fascination with HW, acquired Vindolanda from the Clayton estate. He soon started excavating the site. In 1938, as World War 2 loomed, he placed the site under a protective covenant of guardianship to protect it from pilfering. After the war, his focus shifted to his academic career at Durham University. In 1949, he sold Vindolanda to a farmer, subject to the protective covenant. In the same year, his son, Robin Birley, had undertaken his first series of excavations at the site. In the 1960s, small scale excavations took place at the SW corner of the stone fort and it became clear that larger excavations would reveal much of interest. The then owner of the site was in poor health and, if the land had been sold, there would have been no guarantee that a new owner would have been amenable to excavations. The archaeologists attempted to persuade the owner to sell the land to them but they were unsuccessful. In 1970, Daphne Archibald, the mother of one of Robin Birley's volunteers, managed to buy the land. She donated the grounds of the fort to the Vindolanda Trust.

Soon afterwards, Robin Birley was employed full-time by the trust and serious excavations began outside the walls of the fort. The work was funded largely by visitors' entrance fees and donations. In 1973, the archaeologists made a monumental discovery: in the well-preserved remains of a timber structure, they found the Vindolanda writing tablets. These were letters and documents made from thin sheets of wood which were miraculously still covered in writing. Incredibly, they provided first-hand accounts of life in the fort and have contributed massively to our understanding of Roman life in Britain. It is no exaggeration to state that they are one of the most significant historical finds in Europe. The publicity created by the documents placed Vindolanda in the archaeological limelight and attracted an increasing number of visitors: this generated much revenue to be used for further excavation. Professor Anthony Birley, Robin's son, eventually took the reins, following in the footsteps of his father and grandfather.

The Unmissable Forts of Hadrian's Wall

Vindolanda Roman Fort

Wallsend Roman Fort (Stage 1a)

Wallsend Fort (Segedunum) is managed by Tyne & Wear Archives & Museums and is the most excavated fort along HW. It was cleverly positioned on a plateau overlooking the River Tyne. However, it was not part of the original plan for HW: originally, it was intended that the Wall would terminate further W in what is now Newcastle. The fort was largely destroyed during the Industrial Revolution and houses were built on the site. However, the subsequent decline of industry on the Tyne led to the demolition of many buildings and it was decided to re-expose the fort. Substantial excavations took place during the 1970s and 1980s which enabled detailed mapping of the fort's buildings. Foundations of many buildings are now visible and the museum has artefacts from the fort.

Although no walls of the fort's buildings remain, the site is fascinating because, on the ground, you can see the fort's actual layout. The position of the barrack blocks, commanding officer's house, headquarters, hospital and granaries are visible as well as some walls and gates. You can walk amongst the foundations or get a bird's eye view from the fantastic viewing tower. There is also a replica section of HW and an actual stretch of the Wall's foundations. Unfortunately, the reconstructed bath house was closed at the date of press.

Foundations at Wallsend Roman Fort

Chesters Roman Fort (Stage 3a)

Chesters Fort (Cilurnum) is managed by English Heritage and is one of the best-preserved Roman ruins in Britain. In 1843, John Clayton, the famous protector of HW, inherited the site from his father who had previously turfed over the ruins for aesthetic purposes. John excavated many parts of the fort and established its unmissable museum to display his staggeringly prolific finds from Chesters and other HW sites.

The fort was situated astride HW, guarding the bridge over the River North Tyne. It was occupied by cavalry regiments. The buildings which have been excavated include barrack blocks, the commanding officer's house, the headquarters building and the various gates. However, the bath house steals the show: it is one of the best preserved Roman structures in the world because shortly after it was abandoned, soil from further up the slope covered the building and protected the stone from pilfering. Some of the surviving walls are 3m in height and the changing rooms, steam room, hot room (sauna) and cold room are all visible.

Barracks at Chesters Roman Fort

Housesteads Roman Fort (Stage 3d/3e)

Housesteads Fort (Vercovicium) is owned by the National Trust and managed by English Heritage. It was an infantry fort and has a commanding position on a high ridge. It is probably the best-preserved of all the HW forts having been purchased and protected by John Clayton. Surviving structures include the gates, barracks, headquarters, hospital, commanding officer's house, turret 36b and a latrine, as well as almost all of the fort's external walls. Significantly, it is the only one of the excavated forts that is still physically integrated with visible sections of HW. Accordingly, more than anywhere else on HW, you can picture life as a Roman soldier. The small museum helps too with its model of the fort and artefacts from it.

The north gate at Housesteads Fort

Vindolanda Roman Fort (Stage 3e/4a: off-route)

Vindolanda is owned by the Vindolanda Trust. It was a hinterland fort, positioned a few miles S of HW. It has yielded such rich Roman finds that most HWP walkers will want to visit it. Around CE80, the Romans built the first of a series of timber forts on the site and in the middle of the second century, a stone fort was constructed. It was re-built in the early third century: parts of the external walls, gates, headquarters, latrine and commanding officer's house are still visible. These structures are interesting but not as well-preserved as those at Chesters or Housesteads. This hardly matters though because it is the incredible museum that you will really want to see: it possesses one of the finest collections of Roman artefacts in the world, all of which were found at Vindolanda.

Amongst the items on display are armour, weapons, tools, combs, jewellery, glass, pottery and hundreds of fabulously preserved leather shoes. But the stars of the show are the Vindolanda writing tablets (see page 73) which are probably the most important Roman find in Britain. A few excellent examples of the 2,000 tablets are usually on display: the rest are looked after by the British Museum.

The granaries at Vindolanda Fort

Birdoswald Roman Fort (Stage 4d)

Birdoswald Fort (Banna) is managed by English Heritage. It has an elevated position overlooking the River Irthing: the views from the S of the site are magnificent. The ruins survived because the fort was, for many years, located on working farmland. The walls of the fort, the gates and the granaries have been excavated.

Birdoswald originally lay astride the turf section of HW, with the fort's N walls extending beyond the Wall. When the stone wall replaced the turf wall, the line of HW was altered: the stone wall met the N walls of the fort instead of the side gates further S. It continued to be occupied well into the fifth century, long after the period of Roman rule. The farmhouse on the site was built in 1745.

The wall of Birdoswald Fort runs up to the 18th century farmhouse

Further Reading

- ► **Hadrian's Wall History and Guide** by Guy de la Bédoyère

- ► **Hadrian's Wall** by David J. Breeze & Brian Dobson

- ► **Hadrian's Wall, English Heritage Guidebook** by David Breeze

- ► **Hadrian's Wall: Archaeology and history at the limit of Rome's empire** by Nick Hodgson

- ► **Hadrian's Wall: Everyday Life on a Roman Frontier** by Patricia Southern

- ► **Saving the Wall: The Conservation of Hadrian's Wall** by Stephen Leach & Alan Michael Whitworth

- ► **The Wall: Rome's Greatest Frontier** by Alistair Moffat

- ► **Vindolanda Guide** by Andrew Birley

The trig point at Green Slack, the highest place on the HWP (Stage 4a)

A wonderful view of Broomlee Lough (Stage 3d)

Wallsend/Heddon-on-the-Wall

1

For most of its length, the HWP is a beautiful and fascinating trek. However, most will agree that Stage 1a is not particularly beautiful because it traverses urban Newcastle. Furthermore, other than Segedunum Fort and Newcastle city centre at either end of it, Stage 1a has little to fascinate the trekker. In fact, one reason why many walk E-W is to ensure that they complete the least enjoyable section of the HWP at the start rather than finishing with it. And that makes good sense because the scenery improves progressively as you head W through Section 1. Purists will want to complete Stage 1a so that they have walked the entire HWP, however, others may prefer to start or finish at Newcastle avoiding Stage 1a completely. Whether or not you decide to walk Stage 1a, you should not miss Segedunum Fort in Wallsend, the HWP's E end (see page 74): it is easily accessible from Newcastle by metro or bus (see 'Travel to/from Trail-heads').

The scenery on Stage 1b is better but you still pass through populated areas. However, Stage 1c is much more enjoyable with its rural scenery alongside the River Tyne. For E-W trekkers, Stage 1c is where the HWP starts to come alive. For W-E walkers, the scenery after Stage 1c becomes progressively less interesting all the way to the end.

As regards HW itself, you will see little of it on Section 1 as the HWP does not in fact follow the line of the Wall until the start of Stage 2a. There is a small section of HW at Wallsend and a longer section at Heddon-on-the-

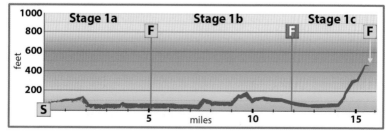

The path along the River Tyne

Wall but that is it, unless you take the Denton Hall Turret Detour (see page 89).

Newcastle itself is a vibrant city and is worth an overnight visit, whether at the start of your trek or for a celebration dinner at the end. There are countless bars, restaurants and shops to occupy your time. And Newcastle Castle is well worth a visit (see page 87).

As its name suggests, the village of Heddon-on-the-Wall is right on HW and its location beside the HWP makes it an excellent place to stay. Accordingly, the available accommodation books up quickly: as an alternative, consider getting a taxi to nearby Wylam where there is more accommodation.

On signposts in the Newcastle area, the HWP is known as 'Hadrian's Way'. Stage 1a is not well marked: there are some signs for 'Hadrian's Cycleway 72' but take care as the cycle path does not always follow the same route as the HWP. Look out for acorns on the lampposts. The markings are better on Stages 1b and 1c.

On Stages 1a and 1b, the route traverses urban areas of Greater Newcastle and it occasionally feels a little 'edgy': incidents involving HWP trekkers are very rare but solo trekkers should exercise caution and stay alert. Do not display expensive cameras and avoid walking these sections late in the day.

		Time	Distance	Ascent	Descent
Stage 1a	Wallsend/Newcastle Swing Bridge	2:00	5.1 miles 8.2km	72ft 22m	98ft 30m
Stage 1b	Newcastle Swing Bridge/Newburn	2:45	6.7 miles 10.7km	184ft 56m	148ft 45m
Stage 1c	Newburn/Heddon-on-the-Wall	1:30	3.6 miles 5.8km	427ft 130m	66ft 20m

Supplies:

Wallsend (Stage 1a) - Asda supermarket on Station Road, near Segedunum Fort

Newcastle (Stage 1a/1b) - supermarkets, shops and ATMs

Lemington (Stage 1b) - pharmacy, newsagents, deli and Asda supermarket

Heddon-on-the-Wall (Stage 1c/2a) - service station and ATM

Wylam (off-route from Stage 1c/2a) - pharmacy, supermarket and ATM

Refreshments/Food:

Crocket's Hotel (Stage 1a)

Café and pub at St Peter's Marina (Stage 1a)

The Tyne Bar (Stage 1a)

Newcastle (Stage 1a/1b)

The Lemington Centre (Stage 1b)

Boat House pub (Stage 1b): closed at the date of press following a fire

Keelman's Lodge pub (Stage 1b/1c)

Heddon-on-the-Wall (Stage 1c/2a) - the Swan & the Three Tuns

Wylam (off-route from Stage 1c/2a)

Accommodation:

Crocket's Hotel (Stage 1a)

Newcastle (Stage 1a/1b)

Keelman's Lodge (Stage 1b/1c)

Heddon-on-the-Wall (Stage 1c/2a)

Wylam (off-route from Stage 1c/2a)

Escape/Access:

Newcastle (Stage 1a/1b)

Lemington (Stage 1b)

Newburn (Stage 1b/1c)

Heddon-on-the-Wall (Stage 1c/2a)

The sculpture of a Roman centurion marks the start/finish of the HWP

E-W

To reach the start from Wallsend Metro station, follow a sign in the station for 'Segedunum'. Head SE, passing under the railway bridge on Station Road. Shortly afterwards, pass Asda Supermarket on the left. At a junction, TR onto Buddle Street: immediately afterwards, cross it and enter the Segedunum Fort car park.

Stage 1a: Wallsend to Newcastle Swing Bridge

S From the sculpture of a Roman centurion in Segedunum car park, head SE following signs for 'Hadrian's Way'. Just afterwards, pass through gates. Immediately afterwards, TR onto a path. Shortly afterwards, pass an original section of HW: it joined the fort to the River Tyne. Keep SH across **Neptune Road** (towards a large image of Hadrian) and climb on a path. 5min later, TL at a fork.

(1) 0:20: Cross Welbeck Road and keep SH on a path between trees. 5min later, pass **Crocket's Hotel** on the right. Keep SH across the next few road junctions.

(2) 0:45: TL at a fork (leaving Hadrian's Cycleway 72). Soon the path zigzags down towards the River Tyne: at the bottom of the slope, TR at a junction and head W along the river bank on a path. 5min later, TL at a junction, remaining beside the river.

(3) 1:20: Cross the lifting bridge at **St Peter's Marina**. Afterwards, bear left back towards the river. Shortly afterwards, TR. Shortly after that, at the **Merchant's Tavern**, TL on Bottlehouse Street. A few minutes later, TR on Glasshouse Street. Shortly afterwards, TL on St Lawrence Road. Soon keep SH on Mariners' Wharf.

(4) 1:45: Shortly after the **Tyne Bar**, TL to reach the river again. 10min later, pass the **Millennium Bridge**: there are plenty of bars and restaurants. 5min later, pass under the **Tyne Bridge**.

F 2:00: Shortly afterwards, arrive at the **Swing Bridge**. A short distance away to the NW, you will find the **Castle Stairs**: take these if you wish to visit **Newcastle Castle** (see box).

W-E

Stage 1a: Newcastle Swing Bridge to Wallsend

F Continue E along the river and pass under the **Tyne Bridge**. 5min later, pass the **Millennium Bridge**: there are plenty of bars and restaurants. 10min later, TL away from the river.

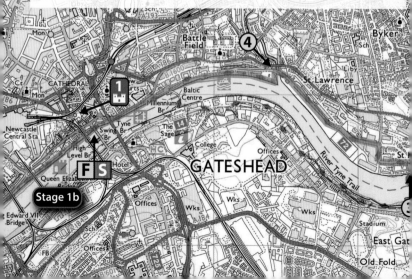

(4) 0:15: Shortly afterwards, TR on Mariners' Wharf. Pass the **Tyne Bar**. After a while, bear left onto St Lawrence Road. TR onto Glasshouse Street. Then TL onto Bottlehouse Street. Shortly afterwards, at the **Merchant's Tavern**, TR on Dobson Crescent. Shortly afterwards, TL along the river.

(3) 0:40: Cross the lifting bridge at **St Peter's Marina**. Then continue alongside the river. 30min later, TL and climb away from the river.

(2) 1:15: TR at a junction onto Hadrian's Cycleway 72. Keep SH across the next few road junctions. Pass **Crocket's Hotel** on the left.

(1) 1:40: Cross Welbeck Road and pick up a path on the other side. Keep SH across Neptune Road (where there is a large image of Hadrian). Eventually, pass an original section of HW: it joined the fort to the River Tyne.

[S] 2:00: Shortly afterwards, TL and enter **Segedunum Fort**. Congratulations! You have completed the HWP.

To reach Wallsend Metro station, exit the fort onto Buddle Street: TR and immediately afterwards, TL onto Station Road. A few minutes later, reach the station on the left.

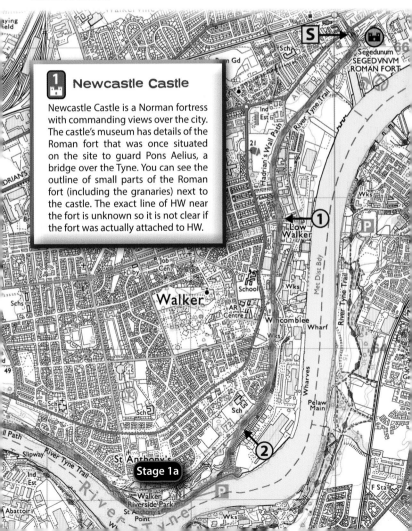

Newcastle Castle

Newcastle Castle is a Norman fortress with commanding views over the city. The castle's museum has details of the Roman fort that was once situated on the site to guard Pons Aelius, a bridge over the Tyne. You can see the outline of small parts of the Roman fort (including the granaries) next to the castle. The exact line of HW near the fort is unknown so it is not clear if the fort was actually attached to HW.

Stage 1a

E-W

Stage 1b: Newcastle Swing Bridge to Newburn

S From the **Swing Bridge**, head SW on a path along the river.

5 1:00: Bear right and drift away from the river on a footpath. Soon continue alongside William Armstrong Drive. A few minutes later, TL and walk alongside Scotswood Road. 5min later, cross the road at traffic lights and continue on the other side. A few minutes later, TR on a path. Soon, keep SH at a junction (no waymark).

6 1:30: Keep SH at a junction. Immediately afterwards, at another junction, bear left. A few minutes later, TR onto Fowberry Road. Shortly afterwards, TL. Shortly after that, TR at a roundabout onto Denton Road. Just afterwards, cross over and continue on the other side. 5min later, TL on a path: afterwards keep to the main path, ignoring offshoots.

7 1:55: TL at a junction and cross a footbridge over the A1: alternatively, TR for the **Denton Hall Turret Detour** (see box). Immediately after the bridge, TL on a path. 5min later, cross Neptune Road: then TR and climb alongside it. 10min later, pass the **Lemington Centre** (which has a café with free WiFi). Shortly afterwards, pass **Lemington**.

8 2:30: TL at a junction. Just afterwards reach Newburn Bridge Road: the village of **Newburn** is on the right. Keep SH across the road onto a tarmac lane. Pass **The Boathouse** pub and then keep SH on a path alongside the river.

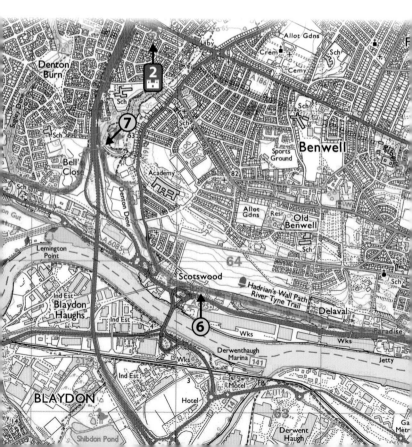

F 2:40: TL, cross a footbridge and arrive at a car park where there is a monument to the Battle of Newburn Ford 1640. TR just before the car park to head to **Keelman's Lodge**: B&B accommodation with a pub at the Big Lamp Microbrewery. Alternatively, to start Stage 1c, head W from the car park on the riverside path.

W-E

Stage 1b: Newburn to Newcastle

F From the car park, head E and cross a footbridge.

8 0:10: Shortly after **The Boathouse** pub, reach Newburn Bridge Road: the village of **Newburn** is on the left. Keep SH across the road onto a path. After a while, pass **Lemington**. Shortly afterwards, pass the **Lemington Centre** (which has a café with free WiFi). 10min later, TL and cross Neptune Road: pick up a path on the other side.

7 0:45: TR at a junction and cross a footbridge over the A1. Immediately afterwards, TR at a junction: alternatively, TL for the **Denton Hall Turret Detour** (see box). Stay on the main path, ignoring offshoots. TR down Denton Road. 5min later, TL at a roundabout onto Fowberry Road. Shortly afterwards, follow the road around to the right. TL on a path.

6 1:10: A few minutes later, keep SH at a fork. Just afterwards TR at a junction onto a path: keep on the main path ignoring offshoots. Eventually, keep SH on a path alongside the Scotswood Road. At traffic lights, cross over the road. Then continue E on the other side. 5min later, TR down William Armstrong Drive.

5 1:40: TL on a path alongside the River Tyne.

S 2:45: Arrive at **Newcastle Swing Bridge**. A short distance away to the NW, you will find **Castle Stairs**: take these if you wish to visit **Newcastle Castle** (see box).

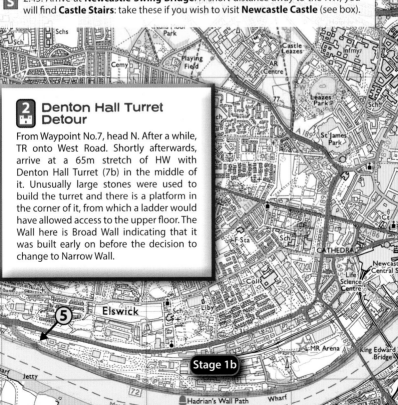

2 Denton Hall Turret Detour

From Waypoint No.7, head N. After a while, TR onto West Road. Shortly afterwards, arrive at a 65m stretch of HW with Denton Hall Turret (7b) in the middle of it. Unusually large stones were used to build the turret and there is a platform in the corner of it, from which a ladder would have allowed access to the upper floor. The Wall here is Broad Wall indicating that it was built early on before the decision to change to Narrow Wall.

Stage 1b

E-W

Stage 1c: Newburn to Heddon-on-the-Wall

S From the car park, continue W on the riverside path.

(9) 0:15: TR at a fork. A few minutes later, TL onto a path.

(10) 0:45: TR onto a path running around the edge of playing fields. At a corner of a playing field, bear left on a tarmac lane heading through a golf course. Soon TL onto a path climbing through trees. After a while, return to the tarmac lane again.

(11) 0:55: TR and climb on a path. After a while, keep SH on a road, passing houses. Soon the road climbs steeply. TR onto Towne Gate. A few minutes after the **Swan Pub**, the road bends left.

(12) 1:25: Shortly afterwards, arrive at Marius Avenue: continue SH on Towne Gate for the **Heddon HW Detour** (see page 96). Otherwise, TL to continue on the HWP: keep SH between houses. Then descend through trees.

F 1:30: Just after a graveyard, TR along a road to reach the **Three Tuns pub**: the **service station** is just E of it.

The Millennium Bridge in Newcastle

W-E

Stage 1c: Heddon-on-the-Wall to Newburn

F From the **Three Tuns pub**, head S along Towne Gate. Shortly afterwards, TL and pass a graveyard. Climb through trees. Soon keep SH between houses.

(12) 0:05: Shortly afterwards, reach Towne Gate again: TL for the **Heddon HW Detour** (see page 96). Otherwise, TR to continue on the HWP. Shortly after the **Swan pub**, TL and descend on Heddon Banks. Eventually, the road becomes a path.

(11) 0:30: TL on a tarmac lane. Soon TR onto a path descending through trees. After a while, TR onto the lane again, heading through a golf course. TR onto a path running around the edge of playing fields.

(10) 0:40: TL onto a track. After a while, TR onto a tarmac lane known as Moore Court.

(9) 1:10: A few minutes later, bear left and head E on a path alongside the River Tyne.

S 1:30: Arrive at a car park where there is a monument to the Battle of Newburn Ford 1640: TL on one of the roads to head to **Keelman's Lodge** (accommodation with a pub at the Big Lamp Microbrewery). Alternatively, to start Stage 1b, continue E on the riverside path.

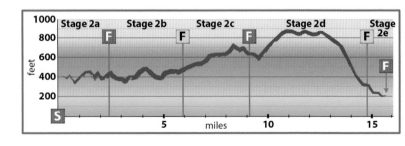

For E-W trekkers, this is where the HWP really starts to shine. You will experience classic Northumberland countryside: a wonderful patchwork of grass and hayfields. And frequently, there is evidence of the Romans' occupation of Britain.

As well as a few excellent stretches of HW, you will pass Brunton Turret, perhaps the finest surviving turret on the whole Wall. Furthermore, often the path runs parallel to clearly visible sections of the Ditch or the Vallum so you will start to understand better their relationship to the Wall itself.

Stage 2a   Stage 2b   Stage 2c   Stage 2d   Stage 2e

1000
800
600
400
200

feet

S

5   miles   10   15

The wonderful section of HW at Brunton Turret

You will also pass the sites of two forts although there is little to see. And at Chollerford, there is the fantastic Chesters Bridge Abutment (½ mile off-route), one of the most important surviving structures of HW.

The Stage is well marked and navigation is straightforward. The terrain is mostly level so there are no big climbs. The paths can be muddy after rain.

		Time	Distance	Ascent	Descent
Stage 2a	Heddon-on-the-Wall/Ironsign	1:00	2.4miles 3.9km	180ft 55m	213ft 65m
Stage 2b	Ironsign/Robin Hood Inn	1:30	3.5miles 5.7km	341ft 104m	262ft 80m
Stage 2c	Robin Hood Inn/ Halton Red House	1:30	3.3miles 5.3km	302ft 92m	164ft 50m
Stage 2d	Halton Red House/ Wall exit	2:30	5.6miles 9.0km	492ft 150m	558ft 170m
Stage 2e	Wall exit/ Chollerford	0:15	0.9miles 1.5km	16ft 5m	52ft 16m

England's famous rolling countryside

Supplies:

Heddon-on-the-Wall (Stage 1c/2a) - service station and ATM

Wylam (off-route from Stage 1c/2a) - pharmacy, supermarket and ATM

Corbridge (2-3 miles off Stage 2d) - supermarket and shops

Hexham (4.5 miles off Stage 2d) - supermarket and shops

Chollerford - the service station/shop has closed down

Humshaugh (0.6 miles N of Chollerford) - village shop

Refreshments/Food:

Heddon-on-the-Wall (Stage 1c/2a) - the Swan & the Three Tuns

Wylam (off-route from Stage 1c/2a)

Robin Hood Inn (Stage 2b/2c)

Vallum Farm Tearoom (Stage 2c)

Matfen High House Restaurant & Micro-brewery (1mile off Stage 2c)

The Errington Coffee House (Stage 2d)

Corbridge (2-3 miles off Stage 2d)

Acomb (2 miles off Stage 2d)

Hexham (4.5 miles off Stage 2d)

Wall (Stage 2d/2e) – Hadrian Hotel

Chollerford (Stage 2e/3a) – George Hotel (closed at date of press) & Riverside Kitchen café

Humshaugh (0.6 miles N of Chollerford) - the Crown Inn

Accommodation:

Heddon-on-the-Wall (Stage 1c/2a)

Wylam (off-route from Stage 1c/2a)

Ironsign Farm B&B (Stage 2a/2b)

Northside Farm Wigwams (½ mile off Stage 2b)

Robin Hood Inn (Stage 2b/2c)

Matfen High House B&B & Dark Sky Glamping (1 mile off Stage 2c)

Well House Farm Campsite (1 mile off Stage 2c)

Halton Red House (Stage 2c/2d)

Corbridge (2-3 miles off Stage 2d)

Acomb (2 miles off Stage 2d)

Hexham (4.5 miles off Stage 2d)

Wall (Stage 2d/2e)

Chollerford (Stage 2e/3a)

Humshaugh (0.6 miles N of Chollerford) - Orchard View B&B

Escape/Access:

Heddon-on-the-Wall (Stage 1c/2a)

Corbridge (2-3 miles off Stage 2d)

Hexham (4.5 miles off Stage 2d)

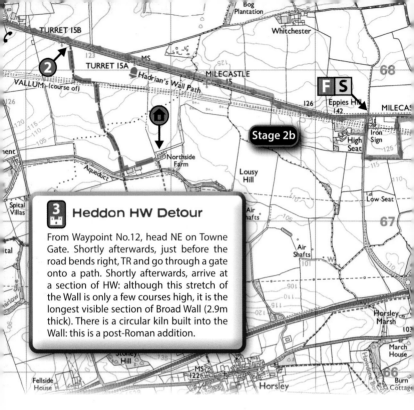

E-W

Stage 2a: Heddon-on-the-Wall to Ironsign

S From the **Three Tuns pub**, head NW on a footpath alongside Military Road. Just after crossing a bridge over the A69 carriageway, TL at a junction: continue on a path (behind a barrier) beside another road. 5min later, TL, go through a gate and descend steps into a field. Immediately afterwards, TR on a path running alongside the road: as you walk, look out for stones from HW in the side of the road embankment.

1 0:35: Cross Stamfordham Road and continue on a grassy path. Pass the grassy site of **Rudchester Fort** (see page 99): only the outline of the fort is visible.

F 0:55: TR onto a small road. A few minutes later, reach **Ironsign Farm B&B**.

Stage 2b: Ironsign to Robin Hood Inn

S Head W on a path alongside Military Road. 10min later, TR, go through a gate and cross the road. Then TL on a path in the Ditch of HW.

2 0:35: Keep SH past the access lane for **Northside Farm Wigwams**. Shortly afterwards, pass the buildings of **Harlow Hill**. A few minutes later, TR and climb steps over a dry-stone wall: then follow a path alongside the road.

3 1:00 : Pass picnic benches at some beautiful reservoirs.

F 1:25: TR and walk along the Military Road. Shortly afterwards, arrive at the **Robin Hood Inn**.

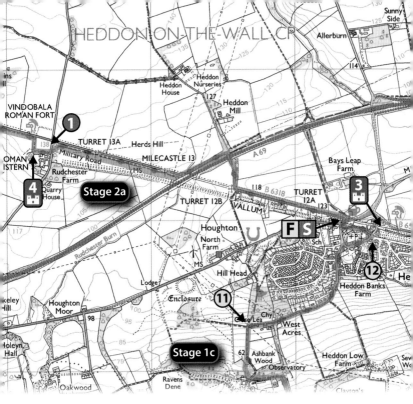

W-E

Stage 2b: Robin Hood Inn to Ironsign

F Walk E along the Military Road. Shortly afterwards TL onto a path.

3 0:30: Pass picnic benches at some beautiful reservoirs. Afterwards, continue E on a path parallel to the road. Climb steps over a dry-stone wall. Then TL along the road. A few minutes later, pass the buildings of **Harlow Hill**.

2 0:55: Keep SH past the access lane for **Northside Farm Wigwams**. Often the path is in the Ditch of HW. TR, cross the road and continue E alongside the Military Road.

S 1:30: 10min later, TR at a junction onto a minor road. Immediately afterwards, reach **Ironsign Farm B&B**.

Stage 2a: Ironsign to Heddon-on-the-Wall

F Head S on the minor road. A few minutes later, TL on a path.

1 0:25: Pass the grassy site of **Rudchester Fort** (see page 99): only the outline of the fort is visible. Shortly afterwards, cross Stamfordham Road. Afterwards, look out for stones from HW in the side of the road embankment. After a while, TL, climb steps and go through a gate. Then TR on a path behind a barrier. TR at a road junction. Immediately afterwards, cross a bridge over the A69 carriageway. Follow the Military Road E.

S 1:00: Reach the **Three Tuns pub** in **Heddon-on-the-Wall**.

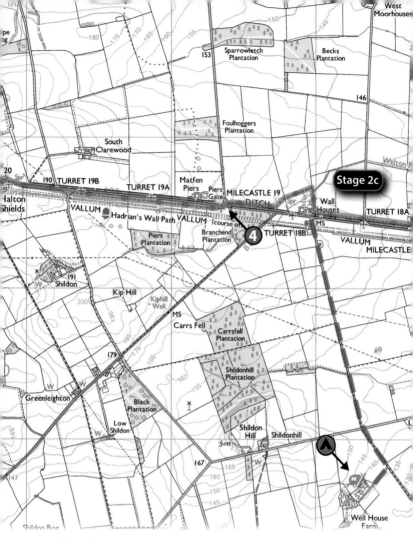

E-W

Stage 2c: Robin Hood Inn to Halton Red House

S At the W side of the inn's car park, pick up a path heading along the Ditch of HW. Shortly afterwards, pass a path on the right which leads to **Matfen High House B&B** and **Dark Sky Glamping**. **Vallum Farm Tearoom** is just across the Military Road. Soon walk alongside the road for 100m. Then TR, cross a bridge over the Ditch and walk on a path beside it. Soon a road on the left leads to **Well House Farm Campsite** (1 mile off-route).

4 0:30: TR along the Military Road. Shortly afterwards, cross the road and pick up a path behind the hedge on the other side. 10min later, TL on a path beside the road again: the path soon crosses the road.

5 1:10: TL, cross the road and climb steps over a wall. Immediately afterwards, TR and continue E. To the left is a clearly visible section of the Vallum. Cross over a hill and descend towards a stile in a dry-stone wall.

F 1:30: Reach **Halton Red House**, an 18th century farm built with stones from HW.

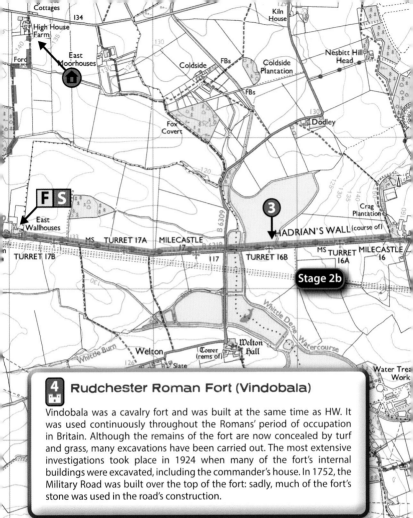

4 Rudchester Roman Fort (Vindobala)

Vindobala was a cavalry fort and was built at the same time as HW. It was used continuously throughout the Romans' period of occupation in Britain. Although the remains of the fort are now concealed by turf and grass, many excavations have been carried out. The most extensive investigations took place in 1924 when many of the fort's internal buildings were excavated, including the commander's house. In 1752, the Military Road was built over the top of the fort: sadly, much of the fort's stone was used in the road's construction.

W-E

Stage 2c: Halton Red House to Robin Hood Inn

F Continue E. After crossing a stile in a dry-stone wall, climb a hill: just to the right is a clearly visible section of the Vallum. Soon after descending the other side of the hill, TL, climb steps over a wall and cross the road.

5 0:20: Immediately afterwards, TR and continue E. After a while, the path crosses the road. Soon it continues behind a hedgerow running parallel to the road.

4 1:00: Cross the road and then TR. Shortly afterwards, pick up a path on the left which runs beside the Ditch of HW. Soon a road on the right leads to **Well House Farm Campsite** (1 mile off-route). After a while, cross a bridge over the Ditch and TL onto the road. After 100m, pick up a path on the left. **Vallum Farm Tearoom** is just across the Military Road. Soon, pass a path on the left which leads to **Matfen High House B&B** & **Dark Sky Glamping**.

S 1:30: Arrive at **Robin Hood Inn**.

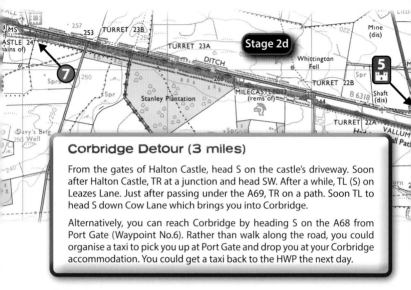

Corbridge Detour (3 miles)

From the gates of Halton Castle, head S on the castle's driveway. Soon after Halton Castle, TR at a junction and head SW. After a while, TL (S) on Leazes Lane. Just after passing under the A69, TR on a path. Soon TL to head S down Cow Lane which brings you into Corbridge.

Alternatively, you can reach Corbridge by heading S on the A68 from Port Gate (Waypoint No.6). Rather than walk along the road, you could organise a taxi to pick you up at Port Gate and drop you at your Corbridge accommodation. You could get a taxi back to the HWP the next day.

E-W

Stage 2d: Halton Red House to Wall exit

S Continue W and 5min later, reach the gates of **Halton Castle** and the site of **Halton Chesters Roman Fort** (Onnum): the fort is unexcavated and there is little to see except grassy mounds. For the **Corbridge Detour** (see box), TL and head S towards Halton Castle. Alternatively, to continue on Stage 2d, head W alongside a dry-stone wall.

6 0:25: At the roundabout at **Port Gate** (see page 103), TL alongside the A68. Just afterwards, TR, cross the A68 into the car park of the **Errington Coffee House**. Climb a stile and continue up a grassy field, with the Vallum clearly visible on the left.

7 1:10: Pass the faint mounds of **Milecastle 24** on the right. Shortly afterwards, climb a stile and cross the road. Then continue W along the Ditch of HW, now on the N side of the Military Road.

8 1:50: TR and cut across a field towards a waymark on a post: alternatively, for the **Acomb/Hexham Detour** (see page 103), TL and cross the Military Road. At the post, continue beside a dry-stone wall.

9 2:05: Cross the road and go down wooden steps. Immediately afterwards, TR to arrive at **Planetrees**, an excellent section of HW (see page 103). Afterwards, cross a stile and continue on a grassy path, running parallel to the road. Soon, TL down a minor road.

F 2:30: Arrive at a road junction: TL to head to **Wall** (5min). Alternatively, to begin Stage 2e, cross the road and TR onto a path beside it.

Stage 2e: Wall exit to Chollerford

S From the junction, head N on the A6079.

10 0:05: TR to view **Brunton Turret** (see page 102). Otherwise, keep SH along the road. 5min later, TL onto Military Road.

F 0:15: Arrive in **Chollerford**. For the **Chesters Bridge Abutment Detour**, see page 105.

100

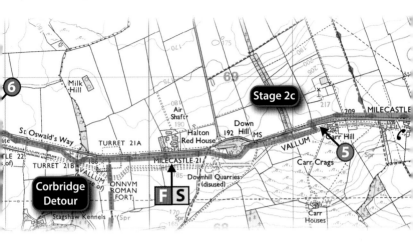

W-E

Stage 2e: Chollerford to Wall exit

F From Chollerford, cross the bridge over the River North Tyne and head SE along Military Road. 5min later, TR onto the A6079.

10 0:10: TL to view **Brunton Turret** (see p102). Otherwise, keep SH along the road.

S 0:15: Arrive at a junction: keep SH to head to **Wall** (5min). Alternatively, TL to begin Stage 2d.

Stage 2d: Wall exit to Halton Red House

F From the junction, head NE on a minor road.15min later, TR onto a path. Soon, reach **Planetrees**, an excellent section of HW (see page 103).

9 0:25: Immediately afterwards, TL, climb wooden steps and cross a road. Then head E on a path.

8 0:40: TR at a post and cut across a field. Shortly afterwards, TL and follow a path E, alongside the Military Road: alternatively, TR and cross the road for the **Acomb/ Hexham Detour** (see page 103). As you continue E, at times you will walk along the Ditch of HW.

7 1:20: Cross the road and a stile. Shortly afterwards, pass the faint mounds of **Milecastle 24** on the left. Soon, climb a stile and head down a grassy field, with the Vallum clearly visible on the right. Cross a stile to enter the car park of the **Errington Coffee House**. TL along the A68.

6 2:05: Shortly afterwards, at the roundabout at **Port Gate** (see page 103), TR onto a path and continue E alongside the Military Road. Eventually, pass the gates of **Halton Castle** and the site of **Halton Chesters Roman Fort** (Onnum): the fort is unexcavated and there is little to see except grassy mounds. For the **Corbridge Detour** (see box), TR and head S towards Halton Castle. Alternatively, to continue on Stage 2d, head E alongside a dry-stone wall.

S 2:30: 5min later, reach **Halton Red House**, an 18th century farmhouse built with stones from HW.

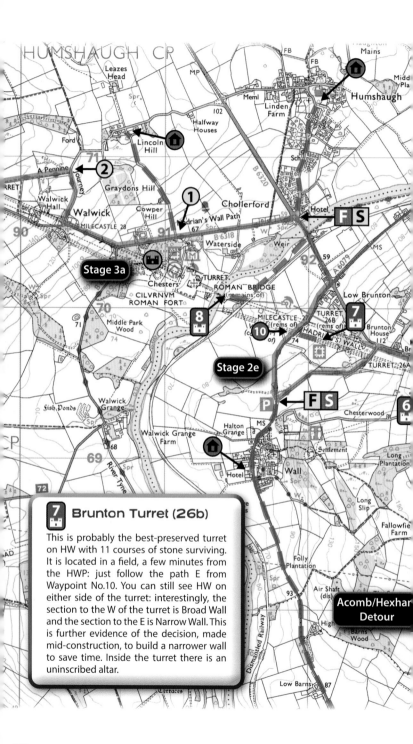

7 Brunton Turret (26b)

This is probably the best-preserved turret on HW with 11 courses of stone surviving. It is located in a field, a few minutes from the HWP: just follow the path E from Waypoint No.10. You can still see HW on either side of the turret: interestingly, the section to the W of the turret is Broad Wall and the section to the E is Narrow Wall. This is further evidence of the decision, made mid-construction, to build a narrower wall to save time. Inside the turret there is an uninscribed altar.

5 Port Gate & Dere Street

Dere Street was the main Roman road into Scotland, running from York at least as far as the Antonine Wall (see page 68). Port Gate was where Dere Street crossed HW. The modern A68 between Corbridge and Port Gate roughly follows the line of Dere Street.

6 Planetrees

This small section of HW is significant because it is partly Broad Wall (2.9m) and partly Narrow Wall (2m), both built upon broad foundations. It is clear evidence of the decision, made mid-construction, to build a narrower wall to save time. The Roman soldiers initially built the foundations of HW about 2.96m wide. They worked W from Newcastle reaching a point 22 Roman miles W of Planetrees. The builders of the Wall's curtain followed in the foundation builders' wake but at a slower speed. The section at Planetrees had only been partly built when the order came to start building the Wall with a reduced gauge.

Planetrees may have been saved from destruction by William Hutton who walked HW end to end in 1801. At Planetrees, a local farmer was dismantling HW to use the stone to build a farmhouse. The farmer had already destroyed substantial sections of the Wall and Hutton's complaints may have helped to save this small section.

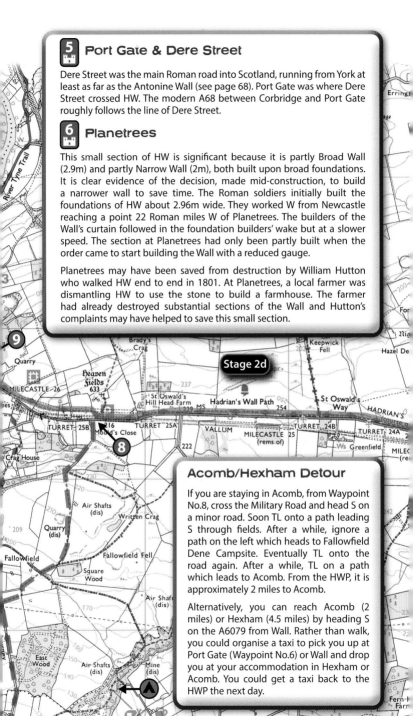

Acomb/Hexham Detour

If you are staying in Acomb, from Waypoint No.8, cross the Military Road and head S on a minor road. Soon TL onto a path leading S through fields. After a while, ignore a path on the left which heads to Fallowfield Dene Campsite. Eventually TL onto the road again. After a while, TL on a path which leads to Acomb. From the HWP, it is approximately 2 miles to Acomb.

Alternatively, you can reach Acomb (2 miles) or Hexham (4.5 miles) by heading S on the A6079 from Wall. Rather than walk, you could organise a taxi to pick you up at Port Gate (Waypoint No.6) or Wall and drop you at your accommodation in Hexham or Acomb. You could get a taxi back to the HWP the next day.

*Chollerford sits beside
the River North Tyne*

8 Chesters Bridge Abutment Detour (½ mile)

If you have the energy, a footpath leads SW from the bridge at Chollerford,
along the E bank of the North Tyne, to Chesters Bridge Abutment. This is one of
the most important sites on HW. The Romans built a large bridge over the river
and the E abutment is still visible with HW itself running into it. Nowadays the
abutment lies slightly away from the river which has moved slightly W over time:
the W abutment has been submerged. The bridge was originally constructed
during Hadrian's reign. However, the E abutment that you see today was built
in the late 2nd century when the original bridge was replaced with a more
ambitious structure. Both bridges were wide enough for carts. Look out for the
phallus carved into one of the stones on the N side of the abutment: the phallus
was considered by the Romans to be a good-luck charm.

Chollerford/Steel Rigg

This is a fabulous section of the HWP. If you are trekking E-W, the scenery becomes increasingly wild and remote: the soft and beautiful farmland gives way to the wild and stark crags of the NNP. The wilder scenery also coincides with the finest and best-preserved parts of HW and this is no accident. The Romans took advantage of the natural highpoints of the terrain by deliberately building the Wall along the steep slopes and cliffs of the crags: the relative inaccessibility of these high places gave HW a degree of protection from destruction and pilfering. The parts of the Wall that remain here are wonderful: long stretches of curtain, many courses high, snake for miles across the undulating slopes. The climax of this section is the remote high ground on Stages 3d and 3e and this is a clear highlight of the entire HWP.

However, the excitement does not end there because the three finest surviving forts of HW are also found within Section 3. They are all completely different and, if time allows it, you would not regret visiting all three. Firstly, there is Chesters Roman Fort (see page 75), just W of Chollerford on Stage 3a with its amazingly well-preserved bath house. Secondly, Vindolanda Roman Fort (see page 77) is only a short distance off-route from Once Brewed (Stage 3e/4a) so if you are staying overnight there, it is little extra effort to visit it: the extensively excavated ruins and

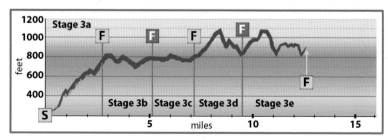

The famous crags in the central section of HW

museum are exceptional. From Once Brewed, you can walk to Vindolanda (1.3 miles) or take the AD122 bus.

However, if you are only intending to visit one fort, then Housesteads Roman Fort (see page 76) is probably the one to choose. This unmissable attraction lies along the route of Stage 3d/3e. Its lofty position offers amazing views over the NNP and the well-preserved ruins, built into HW, provide a great understanding of the internal layout of a Roman fort.

There is a charge to enter each of the forts, however, Chesters Fort is free to members of English Heritage and Housesteads is free to members of English Heritage or the National Trust.

The stage is well marked so navigation is generally straightforward. The terrain in this central section of the HWP is more demanding: there are some longer climbs and descents on the constantly undulating landscape.

		Time	Distance	Ascent	Descent
Stage 3a	Chollerford/Green Carts Farm exit	1:30	2.7 miles 4.3km	571ft 174m	98ft 30m
Stage 3b	Green Carts Farm exit/Carraw B&B	1:15	2.4 miles 3.8km	279ft 85m	180ft 55m
Stage 3c	Carraw B&B/Grindon exit	0:45	2.1 miles 3.4km	82ft 25m	62ft 19m
Stage 3d	Grindon exit/ Housesteads	1:30	2.3 miles 3.7km	522ft 159m	427ft 130m
Stage 3e	Housesteads/Steel Rigg (Once Brewed)	1:45	3.2 miles 5.2km	686ft 209m	673ft 205m

Supplies:

Chollerford (Stage 2e/3a)- none because the service station/shop has closed down

Humshaugh (0.6 miles N of Chollerford) - Village Shop

Refreshments/Food:

Chollerford (Stage 2e/3a) – Riverside Kitchen café & George Hotel

Humshaugh (0.6 miles N of Chollerford) - the Crown Inn

Chesters Fort Café (Stage 3a)

Walwick Hall Hotel (Stage 3a)

Housesteads Fort Café (Stage 3d/3e)

Once Brewed (Stage 3e/4a)

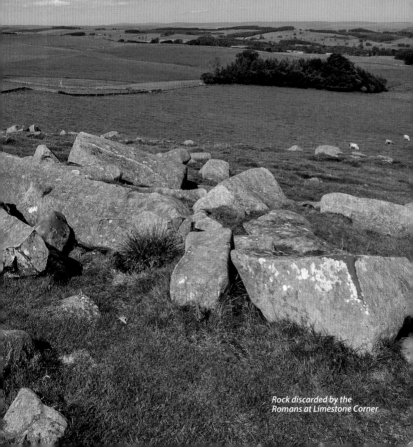

Accommodation:

Chollerford (Stage 2e/3a)

Humshaugh (0.6 miles N of Chollerford) - Orchard View B&B

The Dovecote B&B (½ mile off Stage 3a)

Walwick Hall Hotel (Stage 3a)

Green Carts Farm (Stage 3a/3b)

Hallbarns B&B (1.5 miles off Stage 3b)

Carraw B&B (Stage 3b/3c)

Grindon (5min from Stage 3c/3d) - the Old Repeater Station

Beggar Bog Farm (off-route from Housesteads Fort on Stage 3d/3e)

Once Brewed (Stage 3e/4a)

Escape/Access:

Chesters Fort near Chollerford (Stage 3a)

Brocolitia Fort (Stage 3b)

Housesteads Fort (Stage 3d/3e)

Once Brewed (Stage 3e/4a)

Rock discarded by the Romans at Limestone Corner

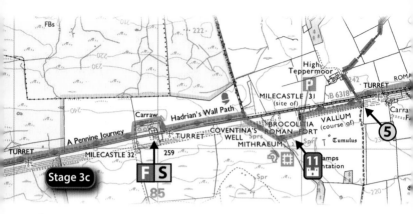

E-W

Stage 3a: Chollerford to Green Carts Farm exit

S From the **Riverside Kitchen** in Chollerford, head W on a footpath beside Military Road (B6318). Soon pass **Chesters Bridge B&B**.

1 0:10: Pass **Chesters Roman Fort** which is one of the highlights of the HWP so take the time to explore it. The exceptional museum contains John Clayton's collection of relics found along HW. Just after the fort, TR on a lane if you are staying at **Dovecote B&B** (½ mile): otherwise continue W alongside the road. 10min later, TR onto a small road, climbing between cottages. Shortly afterwards, pass a stile on the left giving access to **Walwick Hall Hotel**.

2 0:40: TL, cross a stile and head up a grassy path, alongside a fence. 5min later, TR at a fork. Shortly afterwards, you will enter the NNP. Soon, climb a stile and walk alongside the Ditch of HW.

3 1:10: TR along a road. Just afterwards, cross the road and take a path on the left. Alternatively, you can keep SH along the road to access Green Carts Farm, however, the route to Green Carts from the finish of Stage 3a is more enjoyable.

F 1:30: Arrive at **Black Carts**, a fine section of HW with the well-preserved **Turret 29a** (see page 112). Climb alongside the Wall and just afterwards, reach a lane: TR for **Green Carts Farm** or continue SH, and cross the lane, to begin Stage 3b.

Stage 3b: Green Carts Farm exit to Carraw B&B

S From the lane at **Black Carts**, climb a stile and head NW alongside another section of HW.

4 0:20: Continue W past **Limestone Corner** (see page 112), the most northerly point of the entire Roman Empire.

5 0:45: Arrive at a junction: TR to head to **Hallbarns B&B**. To continue on Stage 3b, TL, cross the Military Road and climb steps over a wall. Afterwards, TR on a grassy path. 5min later, arrive at the site of the unexcavated **Carrawburgh Fort** (see page 112): go through a gate to explore it but there is little to see other than grassy mounds. The HWP stays outside the site, heading around the S side of it. Shortly afterwards, TR just before the **Mithraeum** (see page 112), passing around its boundaries. Then cross two stiles. Immediately afterwards, TR at a fork. Soon, cross the Military Road and keep SH on a track. Shortly afterwards, TL and go through a gate.

F 1:15: Arrive at **Carraw B&B**.

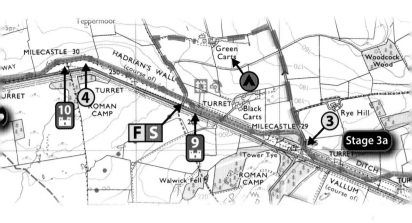

W-E

Stage 3b: Carraw B&B to Green Carts Farm exit

F From **Carraw B&B**, continue E on a path. After 5-10min, go through a gate, cross the Military Road and head SE on a path. A few minutes later, TL and cross two stiles. Then head around the left side of the **Mithraeum** (see page 112). Afterwards, TL and head around the S side of the unexcavated **Carrawburgh Fort** (see page 112): go through a gate at the E side of the fort to explore it but there is little to see other than grassy mounds. From the fort continue E on a path.

(5) 0:30: TL, climb steps over a wall and cross the Military Road. At the other side, keep SH to head to **Hallbarns B&B**. To continue on Stage 3b, TR and head E on a path.

(4) 0:55: Continue E past **Limestone Corner** (see page 112), the most northerly point of the entire Roman Empire. 10-15mins later, descend alongside the **Black Carts** section of HW (see page 112).

S 1:15: Arrive at a lane: TL for **Green Carts Farm** or continue SH and cross the lane to begin Stage 3a.

Stage 3a: Green Carts Farm exit to Chollerford

F From the lane at **Black Carts**, climb a stile and descend SE alongside a fine section of HW with the well-preserved **Turret 29a** (see page 112).

(3) 0:20: TR along a road. Just afterwards, cross the road and take a path on the left. Soon walk alongside the Ditch of HW. You will shortly be leaving the NNP. Keep SH at a junction.

(2) 0:50: Cross a stile and TR onto a small road. Soon pass a stile on the right giving access to **Walwick Hall Hotel**. Shortly afterwards, TL and descend on the Military Road. Shortly before Chesters Fort, TL on a lane if you are staying at **Dovecote B&B** (½ mile): otherwise continue E alongside the road.

(1) 1:20: Pass **Chesters Roman Fort** which is one of the highlights of the HWP. The exceptional museum contains John Clayton's collection of relics found along HW. A few minutes later, pass **Chesters Bridge B&B**.

S 1:30: Arrive in **Chollerford**. For the **Chesters Bridge Abutment Detour**, see page 105.

Black Carts

Black Carts is a 200m section of Narrow Wall. However, Turret 29a was designed and built for the originally planned Broad Wall, before the decision was taken to build with a reduced width. That is why the turret has 'wing' walls (designed to integrate with Broad Wall) which were left exposed when the Narrow Wall was linked to the turret.

Just to the N, the Ditch is clearly visible. The site was first excavated by John Clayton in 1873: he found three 'centurial' stones showing names of the soldiers that built the section of Wall. The stones are on display in the museum at Chesters Fort. Further excavations took place in 1971.

 ## Limestone Corner

At Limestone Corner there is a section of unfinished Ditch filled with abandoned stone blocks: one slab still shows the holes chiselled by the Romans to split the rock. The stone here is hard basalt and it appears that the Roman masons found it too hard to work with. Accordingly, they gave up trying to complete this part of the Ditch although the Vallum to the S was finished and is still visible.

 ## Carrawburgh Roman Fort (Brocolitia), the Mithraeum & Coventina's Well

Brocolitia was not part of the original HW scheme. It was probably built around CE130: the Vallum here was already constructed and was filled in so that the fort could be built on top of it.

There is an excavated temple to Mithras (known as a 'Mithraeum') at the SW corner of the fort. It was discovered in 1949 when a drought caused the stonework to show above the ground. Mithras was a Persian warrior god who was thought to provide strength to his worshippers. The cult was exclusive to males and appealed to Roman soldiers. Mithraea were sunk into the ground and had no windows. Following excavation, the original altars and statues were replaced with replicas: the originals are in the Museum of Antiquities in Newcastle.

Coventina's Well, located just W of the fort, was a shrine to the water goddess Coventina. Nothing is visible today except a small pool where the sacred spring rose from the ground. The spring was recorded in 1732 but its location was lost. It was found again by lead-miners in 1876. When John Clayton heard about the find, he ordered his men to explore. They removed large stones from the top of the pool and discovered a horde of treasure: altars, sculptures, pottery, jewellery and more than 13,000 coins. Sadly, the coins were melted down to make an eagle weighing 6.5kg.

 ## Coesike Turret (33b)

Turret 33b was first excavated in 1935. The surviving ruins are up to 1.1m high so you can clearly see its dimensions. The broad wing walls are clearly visible where the Narrow Wall meets it on either side. The turret was permanently abandoned by the Romans in the late 2nd century. There is no evidence of a door (which must have been blocked up).

 ## Milecastle 35

External and internal walls of Milecastle 35 are still visible. Notably there is no N gate through HW: this may be because there was such a steep drop to the N or perhaps it was blocked up at a later date.

Turret 35a

Turret 35a was only used by the Romans for about 80 years. Changes to the overall scheme of HW reduced the usefulness of the turrets. This one was demolished in the early 3rd century and HW was built over it.

 ## Knag Burn Gate

Normally, the gateways in HW were located within milecastles or forts. However, Knag Burn Gate is situated on the outside of Housesteads Fort. It was probably built for convenience but it is not clear when. It would have been easier for traffic to pass through Knag Burn Gate (which is situated in a valley) rather than having to climb up the slope to the fort's gates and back down the other side. The Knag Burn (a stream) passed through a culvert under HW.

In fact, the structure eventually had two gates with a passageway in-between: traffic would presumably have passed through the first gate for examination by the soldiers. Then, once cleared for passage, the 2nd gate would have been opened, allowing access through the Wall.

 ## Milecastle 37

The internal and external walls of this well-preserved milecastle are still visible. To the E are the soldiers' barracks which would probably have garrisoned eight men. Significantly, some of the N gate's arch stones are still in place, so you can easily picture their appearance in Roman times. The fact that there is a gate at all is interesting too: the terrain slopes steeply to the N so the gate cannot have been very useful.

 ## Sycamore Gap

At Sycamore Gap, HW crosses a saddle with a prominent sycamore tree in the middle of it. The iconic tree in the gap has risen to fame in recent years after it was used in a variety of films and TV programmes, including Robin Hood, Prince of Thieves which starred Kevin Costner. It is possibly the most photographed site on HW.

 ## Castle Nick (Milecastle 39)

This milecastle gets its name from its location within a 'nick' in the crags. Inside you can see the remains of barracks and other buildings. It was built using Narrow Wall dimensions, however, Broad Wall foundations were prepared along part of its N wall. There are few visible turrets in this area because many were demolished by the Romans from the late 2nd century onwards. Furthermore, it is thought that remaining stones from the turrets were used by John Clayton to rebuild the curtain of HW in the 19th century.

 ## Peel Gap Tower

The tower in Peel Gap was discovered in 1986. It is located halfway between Turrets 39a and 39b in what was probably a weak spot along HW: the tower may have been built as an extra turret to 'plug' Peel Gap. Furthermore, although it was rare for the Romans to depart from the rigid system of fixed distances between milecastles and turrets on HW, the distance between turrets 39a and 39b is longer than usual: almost ½ Roman mile instead of ⅓. So perhaps this necessitated an additional turret. The tower was built onto the existing curtain of HW, indicating that it was built later (possibly around the same time as the forts along the Wall).

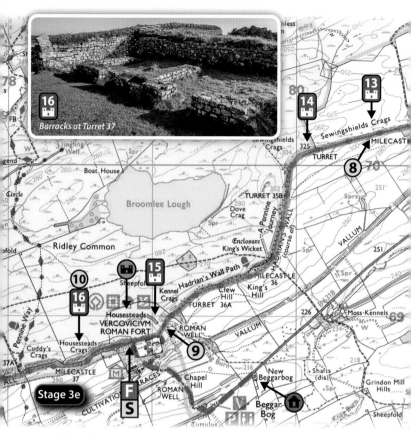

Barracks at Turret 37

E-W

Stage 3c: Carraw B&B to Grindon exit

S From Carraw B&B, head W on a path which runs parallel to the N side of the Military Road. Pass **Milecastle 33** which is little more than a mound.

F 0:45: Shortly before the Military Road bends sharply left, arrive at a stile providing access to the road near **Grindon**: to head to the **Old Repeater Station** (5min), cross the stile and TR along the road. Alternatively, continue W on the path to begin Stage 3d.

Stage 3d: Grindon exit to Housesteads Fort

S Continue W on the path. A few minutes later, pass **Coesike Turret (33b)**: see page 112.

6 0:10: Pass the site of **Grindon Milecastle (34)** at a clump of trees enclosed by a stone wall. 5min later, pass **Grindon Turret (34a)** which sits behind a stone wall.

7 0:20: Keep SH across a track and enter woodland. A few minutes later, exit from the trees to arrive at the start of **Sewingshields Crags**: climb alongside HW. This is the start of a series of long sections of HW which cling to the tops of the crags and cliffs: a clear highlight of the HWP. The Wall here is Narrow Wall on broad foundations.

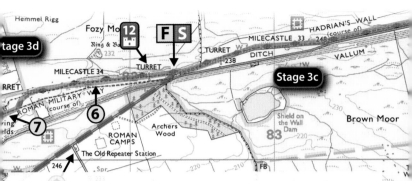

(8) 0:40: Continue climbing past **Milecastle 35** (see page 112). 5-10min later, pass **Turret 35a** (see page 113). Shortly afterwards, the path bends towards the S: when HW peters out, follow a more recent dry-stone wall. This undulating section is tiring but the views are magnificent.

(9) 1:25: Just before Housesteads Fort, HW appears again: cross a dry-stone wall just to the left of HW, using stone steps. Then walk along the left side of the Wall. Shortly afterwards, TR through **Knag Burn Gate** (see page 113). Immediately afterwards, TL and continue uphill to the right of HW.

F 1:30: 5min later, reach a gate at the NW corner of the unmissable **Housesteads Roman Fort**: pass through the gate and descend S to reach the ticket office, café and museum. Alternatively, keep SH to begin Stage 3e.

W-E

Stage 3d: Housesteads Fort to Grindon exit

F From the NW corner of the fort, descend E along its N wall. After 5min, TR through **Knag Burn Gate** (see page 113). Immediately afterwards, TL and continue uphill to the right of HW.

(9) 0:05: Shortly afterwards, cross a dry-stone wall (just to the right of HW) using stone steps. Then climb through trees. Soon exit from the trees and continue across the famous **Sewingshields Crags**, a clear highlight of the HWP. This undulating section is tiring but the views are magnificent. Follow a dry-stone wall upwards to the N. When the path bends to the E, HW appears again. Shortly afterwards, pass **Turret 35a** (see page 113).

(8) 0:50: Descend past **Milecastle 35** (see page 112). Here HW is Narrow Wall on broad foundations. Eventually, enter woodland.

(7) 1:10: A few minutes later, exit from the trees. Shortly afterwards, keep SH across a track and continue E on a path: alternatively, TR down the track for an alternative route to **Grindon**. A few minutes later, pass **Grindon Turret (34a)** which sits behind a stone wall.

(6) 1:20: Pass the site of **Grindon Milecastle (34)** at a clump of trees enclosed by a stone wall. Soon pass **Coesike Turret (33b)**: see page 112.

S 1:30: A few minutes later, shortly after the Military Road bends sharply right, arrive at a stile providing access to the road: to head to the **Old Repeater Station** near **Grindon** (5min), cross the stile and TR along the road. Alternatively, continue E on the path to begin Stage 3c.

Stage 3c: Grindon exit to Carraw B&B

F From the stile, continue E on a path. Pass **Milecastle 33** which is little more than a mound.

S 0:45: Arrive at **Carraw B&B**.

115

207

Stage 4a

Stage 3e: Housesteads Fort to Steel Rigg

S From the gate at the NW corner of the fort, head W on a clear path: just to the right, there is a path on top of HW but walking on the Wall is now discouraged. You will notice that the Wall here is topped with turf and there is no mortar between the facing stones: this part of HW was repaired under John Clayton in the 19th century (see page 72).

10 0:10: Pass **Milecastle 37** (see page 113). 5-10min later, go through a gate and keep SH uphill: this is where the Pennine Way joins the HWP. The path now heads along the magnificent **Hotbank Crags** with fantastic stretches of HW which were repaired by John Clayton.

11 0:50: Descend to the site of **Hotbank Milecastle (38)**, which is just beside Hotbank Farm. A few minutes later, go through a pair of gates and continue on the right of a dry-stone wall. Soon enter woods. After exiting the trees, walk along the sublime **Highshield Crags** with amazing views of **Crag Lough** and the NNP: take care as the drops are sheer.

12 1:15: Soon after HW reappears again, descend into the famous **Sycamore Gap** (see page 113). Pass through the gap and then TR, climbing steeply. Shortly after reaching the top of the slope, pass two 16th century shepherds' huts. Shortly afterwards, pass **Castle Nick (Milecastle 39)**: see page 113. Continue along Peel Crags.

13 1:40: Descend steeply on stone steps into **Peel Gap** where there are the remains

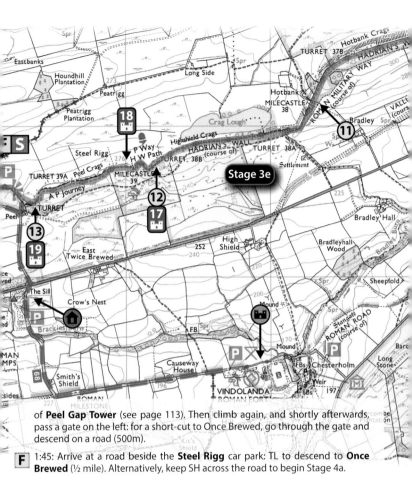

of **Peel Gap Tower** (see page 113). Then climb again, and shortly afterwards, pass a gate on the left: for a short-cut to Once Brewed, go through the gate and descend on a road (500m).

F 1:45: Arrive at a road beside the **Steel Rigg** car park: TL to descend to **Once Brewed** (½ mile). Alternatively, keep SH across the road to begin Stage 4a.

W-E

Stage 3e: Steel Rigg to Housesteads Fort

F From the road beside Steel Rigg car park, head E on a path. Shortly afterwards, descend into **Peel Gap** where there are the remains of **Peel Gap Tower** (see page 113). Then climb steeply on stone steps. Head along Peel Crags: this part of HW was repaired by John Clayton in the 19th century. Eventually, pass **Castle Nick (Milecastle 39)**: see page 113. Shortly, pass two 16th century shepherds' huts.

12 0:30: Just afterwards, descend into the famous **Sycamore Gap** (see page 113). Pass through it and then TR, climbing steeply. Head along the sublime Highshield Crags with amazing views of **Crag Lough** and the NNP: take care as the drops are sheer. Soon enter woods. After exiting the trees, go through a pair of gates.

11 0:50: A few minutes later, pass the site of **Hotbank Milecastle (38)**, which is just beside Hotbank Farm. Afterwards, climb up **Hotbank Crags** with its fantastic stretches of HW. After 35mins, go through a gate and keep SH uphill: this is where the Pennine Way joins the HWP.

10 1:35: After 10min, pass **Milecastle 37** (see page 113).

S 1:45: Reach a gate at the NW corner of the unmissable **Housesteads Roman Fort**: pass through the gate and descend S to reach the ticket office, café and museum. Alternatively, to begin Stage 3d, head E along the N wall of the fort.

117

Sewingshields Crags

4

Steel Rigg (Once Brewed)/Lanercost exit

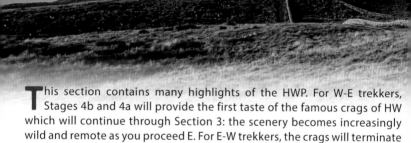

This section contains many highlights of the HWP. For W-E trekkers, Stages 4b and 4a will provide the first taste of the famous crags of HW which will continue through Section 3: the scenery becomes increasingly wild and remote as you proceed E. For E-W trekkers, the crags will terminate towards the end of Stage 4b, leading into the wonderfully green farmland that continues practically all the way to the end of the trek.

As with Section 3, the wilder scenery coincides with the finest and best-preserved parts of HW: the relative inaccessibility of these high places gave HW a degree of protection from destruction and pilfering. The parts of HW that remain here are wonderful: long, many courses high and snaking for miles across the undulating slopes.

W of the River Irthing (Stage 4d), HW is generally not as well-preserved as it is to the E, however, there are still some excellent stretches. The eagle-eyed trekker should notice that the sections just to the E of the River Irthing were built as Narrow Wall on broad foundations whereas all sections to the W of it were Narrow Wall on narrow foundations.

There are plenty of milecastles and turrets on display: Cawfields Milecastle (42), Mucklebank Turret (44b) and Poltross Burn Milecastle (48) are arguably the most interesting. And there are forts too: on Stage 4d, you pass Birdoswald Roman Fort (see page 78) which is worth a visit, although there is less to see than at the forts of Housesteads, Chesters and

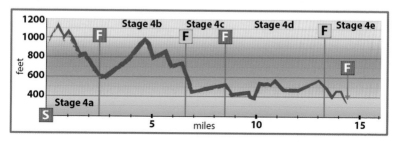

Winshield Crags (Stage 4a)

Vindolanda. Furthermore, Stage 4a passes close to Vindolanda Roman Fort with its staggering museum (see page 77). The best way to access it is from Once Brewed (Stage 3e/4a): you can walk from there (1.3 miles) or take the AD122 bus.

Although it is a short distance off the HWP on Stage 4e, Lanercost Priory (see page 131) is a highlight of the HWP and it has relevance to HW too: it was built partly from stones robbed from the Wall. The buildings are open to visitors and the grounds of the priory, which run down to the River Irthing, are wonderful. It is a fabulous experience to combine a priory visit with an overnight stay at Abbey Farm (which is within the walls of the priory).

The section is well marked so navigation is generally straightforward. The terrain in this central section of the HWP is more demanding: there are some longer climbs and descents on the constantly undulating landscape.

		Time	Distance	Ascent	Descent
Stage 4a	Steel Rigg (Once Brewed)/Cawfields Quarry	1:15	2.5miles 4.1km	328ft 100m	673ft 205m
Stage 4b	Cawfields Quarry/ Holmhead	1:45	4.1miles 6.6km	712ft 217m	869ft 265m
Stage 4c	Holmhead/Gilsland	0:45	1.9miles 3.1km	131ft 40m	197ft 60m
Stage 4d	Gilsland/Banks	2:15	4.8miles 7.8km	502ft 153m	525ft 160m
Stage 4e	Banks/Lanercost exit	0:30	1.1miles 1.7km	121ft 37m	279ft 85m

Supplies:

Hadrian's Wall Campsite (0.8 miles off Stage 4a) - small shop

Cawfields Quarry car park (Stage 4a/4b) – water tap

Haltwhistle (3 miles off Stage 4a/4b) – supermarkets and shops

Walltown Quarry (Stage 4b) – small shop selling drinks

Slack House Farm (0.6 miles off Stage 4d) – farm shop

Refreshments/Food:

Once Brewed (Stage 3e/4a)

Milecastle Inn (½ mile off Stage 4a)

Haltwhistle (3 miles off Stage 4a/4b)

Roman Army Museum tea room (near Walltown Quarry car park on Stage 4b)

Greenhead – Greenhead Hotel & Ye Olde Forge Tea Room (0.4 miles off Stage 4c)

Gilsland (Stage 4c/4d) – House of Meg café, the Samson Inn & the Bridge Inn

Birdoswald Fort café (Stage 4d)

Haytongate Farm (Stage 4e) – unmanned snack hut

Lanercost Tea Room (½ mile off Stage 4e)

Cawfields Milecastle 42
(Stage 4a)

Accommodation:

Once Brewed (Stage 3e/4a)

Winshields Campsite (½ mile off Stage 4a): can be accessed from Stage 4a or from Once Brewed

Hadrian's Wall Campsite (0.8 miles off Stage 4a)

Bridge House B&B (½ mile off Stage 4a)

Herding Hill Farm (1 mile off Stage 4a)

Haltwhistle (3 miles off Stage 4a/4b)

Walltown Lodge B&B (Stage 4b)

Holmhead Guest House (Stage 4b/4c)

Greenhead (0.4 miles off Stage 4c)

Hadrian's Holiday Lodges B&B (0.4 miles off Stage 4c)

Gilsland (Stage 4c/4d)

Willowford Farm B&B (Stage 4d)

Slack House Farm (0.6 miles off Stage 4d)

Banks (Stage 4d/4e) - Quarryside Campsite

Haytongate Barn (Stage 4e)

Lanercost Priory (½ mile off Stage 4e/5a)

Escape/Access:

Once Brewed (Stage 3e/4a)

Haltwhistle (3 miles off Stage 4a/4b)

Walltown Quarry (Stage 4b)

Gilsland (Stage 4c/4d)

Birdoswald Fort (Stage 4d)

Banks (Stage 4d/4e)

Lanercost Priory (off-route from Stage 4e/5a)

E-W

Stage 4a: Steel Rigg to Cawfields Quarry

S From the road beside the Steel Rigg car park, climb W alongside a dry-stone wall onto **Winshield Crags**. After 10-15min, the dry-stone wall gives way to a beautiful section of HW.

1 0:20: Reach the trig point at **Green Slack (345m)**: this is the highest point on HW and is roughly halfway along the HWP. A few minutes later, pass a path on the left which leads to **Winshields Campsite** (½ mile).

2 0:45: Keep SH across a small road at **Caw Gap**: alternatively, TL and head S on a path to head to **Hadrian's Wall Campsite**. Continue upwards, alongside HW again, onto **Cawfield Crags**. Shortly afterwards, pass **Turret 41a** (see box). As you continue, look out for the Vallum below to the S.

3 1:10: At the W side of **Cawfields Milecastle 42** (see box), TR at a junction, descending through a gate onto a track: alternatively, TL to head to the **Milecastle Inn**, **Bridge House B&B** and **Herding Hill Farm**. Just afterwards, TL onto a path. Shortly afterwards, pass **Cawfields Lake**.

F 1:15: Arrive at **Cawfields Quarry** car park: there are picnic benches, a toilet and a water tap.

 ### Turret 41a

Evenly spaced turrets were part of the original scheme for HW. However, after forts were built along the Wall, the turrets became less useful. Many, like Turret 41a, were therefore demolished. All that is left here are its foundations. Originally, it was recessed into HW but, after it was destroyed, the recess was blocked up: this is still visible.

 ### Cawfields Milecastle (42)

Fortunately, Milecastle 42 survived the extensive quarrying which took place in this area in the early 20th century. Unusually, it was built partly using Broad Wall measurements and partly using Narrow Wall measurements. None of the internal buildings are visible but the walls and gateway are well-preserved: the robust masonry may indicate that it had a gate-tower. The milecastle was built on a slope even though there is a flat site just to the W. Some believe that this is explained by the Romans' bureaucratic devotion to the rigid measurements of Hadrian's system for the Wall: Milecastle 42 is exactly 1 Roman mile from the next milecastles to the E and W. However, the flat site is in a dip, restricting visibility, so in fact, Milecastle 42 may have been strategically sited to ensure better views over the surrounding countryside.

 ### Great Chesters Roman Fort (Aesica)

This was originally the site of Milecastle 43 which was built to Broad Wall measurements. However, after the decision was taken to build forts along HW, the milecastle was demolished and the fort was built in its place, with Narrow Wall at either side. Parts of the headquarters building and the original stone of the W gate are still visible. Perhaps the most interesting aspect of the fort is the altar at the S gate which bears a carving of a jug (see image): this is the only original altar left standing on HW.

W-E

Stage 4a: Cawfields Quarry to Steel Rigg

F Head NE from the toilet block and pick up a path heading around the left side of **Cawfields Lake**. A few minutes later, TR onto a track.

3 0:05: Just afterwards, climb through a gate. Then TL and pass **Cawfields Milecastle (42)**: see box. Afterwards, climb alongside HW onto **Cawfield Crags**: as you continue, look out for the Vallum below to the S. Descend past **Turret 41a** (see box).

2 0:35: Shortly afterwards, descend to a small road at **Caw Gap**: TR and head S on a path to head to **Hadrian's Wall Campsite**. To continue on Stage 4a, climb NE. Pass a path on the right which leads to **Winshields Campsite** (½ mile).

1 1:00: A few minutes later, reach the trig point at **Green Slack (345m)**: this is the highest point on HW and is roughly halfway along the HWP. Descend alongside a beautiful section of HW.

S 1:15: Arrive at a road beside the **Steel Rigg** car park: TR to descend to **Once Brewed** (½ mile). Alternatively, keep SH across the road to begin Stage 3e.

---

23 Mucklebank Turret (44b)

The sublime elevated location makes Turret 44b (see image below) one of our favourite places on HW. The views over the surrounding landscape are magnificent and it is easy to imagine life as a soldier tasked with surveillance of the countryside below. Unusually, the turret is built into a corner of HW.

24 Turret 45a

Situated high on Walltown Crags, Turret 45a (see image) has some of the best views on HW. The Wall's foundations run seamlessly through the turret, however, above the foundations, the Wall and the turret are separate structures, meeting with straight joins. Furthermore, there are no wing walls and the Wall meets the turret at an angle, suggesting that they were built separately. Some believe therefore that Turret 45a was built before the Wall curtain and was originally used as a free-standing signal tower.

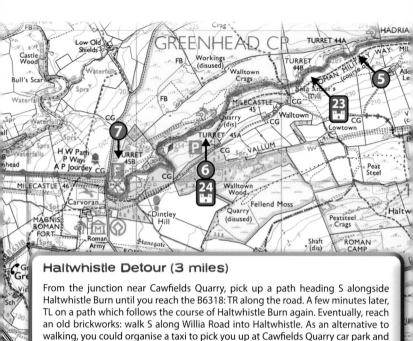

Haltwhistle Detour (3 miles)

From the junction near Cawfields Quarry, pick up a path heading S alongside Haltwhistle Burn until you reach the B6318: TR along the road. A few minutes later, TL on a path which follows the course of Haltwhistle Burn again. Eventually, reach an old brickworks: walk S along Willia Road into Haltwhistle. As an alternative to walking, you could organise a taxi to pick you up at Cawfields Quarry car park and drop you at your Haltwhistle accommodation. You could get a taxi back to the HWP the next day.

E-W

Stage 4b: Cawfields Quarry to Holmhead B&B

S Head N from the toilet block in the car park and TL onto a road. Shortly, reach a junction: for the **Haltwhistle Detour** (see box), pick up a path heading S. Alternatively, to continue on Stage 4b, TR on a lane and cross a bridge. Shortly afterwards, TL, climb a stone stile and continue uphill on a grassy path. Then climb alongside a dry-stone wall: notice the Ditch of HW on the right.

4 0:20: At a farm, cross a stile and keep SH towards the corner of a dry-stone wall. Just afterwards, pass the ruins of **Great Chesters Fort** (see page 124).

5 0:50: TR at a faint fork, crossing a stone stile: ignore the wooden stile on the left. 5-10min later, descend past **Mucklebank Turret (44b)**: see page 125. Soon, at the bottom of the slope, cross a stile. Then bear left, climbing across the grassy slopes of **Walltown Crags**. As you head SW, there are a variety of paths: stay high for the best views.

6 1:15: Pass **Turret 45a** (see page 125) set in a magnificent stretch of HW. When HW ends at a more recent dry-stone wall, TL and follow the dry-stone wall downhill. A few minutes later, TR through a gate. Immediately afterwards, TR at a junction. 5min later, TL at a fork beside a beautiful lake with picnic benches.

7 1:30: Soon, keep SH through **Walltown Quarry** car park: there are toilets, an information centre and a small shop. TR onto a road: alternatively, TL for the interesting **Roman Army Museum** and **Walltown Lodge B&B** which are only a few minutes away. Shortly afterwards, TL on a path which soon descends just to the N of the Ditch of HW. After a while, cross a stile and descend on a clear path.

F 1:45: The path passes below **Thirlwall Castle**. Just afterwards, arrive at **Holmhead Guest House**.

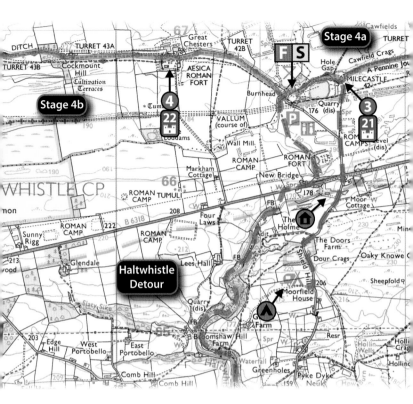

W-E

Stage 4b: Holmhead to Cawfields Quarry

F From Holmhead Guest House, head E and soon climb. A few minutes later, cross a stile and climb on a path just to the N of the Ditch of HW. After a while, TR on a minor road. Shortly afterwards, TL: alternatively, keep SH for the **Roman Army Museum** and **Walltown Lodge B&B** which are only a few minutes away.

7 0:15: Keep SH through **Walltown Quarry** car park: there are toilets, an information centre and a small shop. Follow a path heading around the N side of a beautiful lake. 5min later, go through a gate and TL: climb alongside a dry-stone wall. When you meet HW, follow it upwards.

6 0:35: Pass **Turret 45a** (see page 125) set in a magnificent stretch of HW. As you continue NE, there are a variety of paths: stay high for the best views. Soon descend and cross a stile. Then keep SH and climb past **Mucklebank Turret (44b)**: see page 125.

5 1:00: 5-10min later, cross a stone stile: ignore the wooden stile on the right. Then continue E.

4 1:25: Pass the ruins of **Great Chesters Fort** (see page 124). Afterwards, cross a stile and continue E, alongside a wall: notice the Ditch of HW on the left. Just after passing a house, cross a stile. Immediately afterwards, TR on a lane, cross a bridge and reach a junction: for the **Haltwhistle Detour** (see box), pick up a path heading S. Alternatively, to continue on Stage 4b, TL on the road.

S 1:45: Shortly afterwards, TR into **Cawfields Quarry** car park: there are picnic benches, a toilet and a water tap.

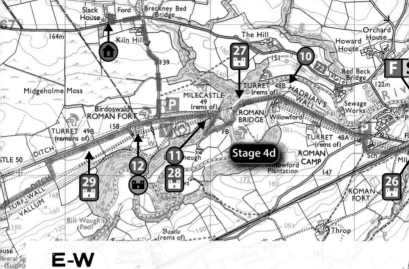

E-W

Stage 4c: Holmhead to Gilsland

S From Holmhead Guest House, head W. Immediately afterwards, cross a footbridge. Afterwards, climb briefly on a track beside **Thirlwall Castle** (see box). At an information board, TL on a path.

8 0:05: Soon reach a junction. TL for the **Greenhead Detour** (see box): alternatively, to continue on Stage 4c, keep SH and cross a bridge. Just afterwards, cross train tracks when the light is green: look both ways. Shortly afterwards, TR along a busy road. Soon pass a surviving piece of HW emerging from the road embankment. Shortly afterwards, TL on a path to continue on Stage 4c: alternatively, keep SH for **Hadrian's Holiday Lodges B&B** (0.4 miles). The path runs along the line of HW and you can make out the shape of the Vallum in places.

9 0:25: TR onto a lane. Shortly afterwards, at a bend, keep SH on a path. Head through **Gap Farm**. Then TL onto a road. Shortly afterwards, TL on a path.

F 0:45: Arrive at a junction beside a tunnel: to start Stage 4d, keep SH. To head to Gilsland, TR and go through the tunnel. A few minutes later, reach the main street of **Gilsland**.

 Thirlwall Castle

The castle was built in the early 14th century by John Thirlwall, using stone from HW. During the 15th and 16th centuries, it provided defence against raids from across the border with Scotland. It was abandoned by the Thirlwall family in the 17th century. Through the subsequent centuries, its condition deteriorated as the stone was pilfered for other building works. In 1999, Northumberland National Park Authority acquired the ruins.

26 **Poltross Burn Milecastle (48)**

This is one of the best-preserved milecastles on HW. It is bigger than usual and inside there are the remains of two barrack blocks. Broad Wall foundations on the E wing indicate that it was built (at least partly) before the decision was taken to narrow the width of HW. In the NW corner there are the remains of ovens. It is the only milecastle with surviving steps: these probably led to the ramparts.

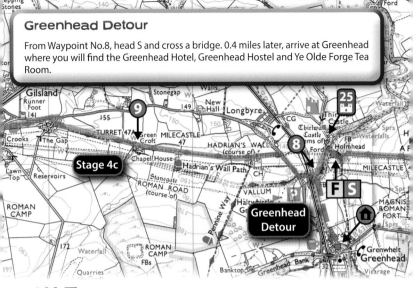

Greenhead Detour

From Waypoint No.8, head S and cross a bridge. 0.4 miles later, arrive at Greenhead where you will find the Greenhead Hotel, Greenhead Hostel and Ye Olde Forge Tea Room.

W-E

Stage 4c: Gilsland to Holmhead

F From the junction beside the tunnel at the end of Stage 4d, head NE. Just afterwards, TR on a path. After a while, TR on a road. Shortly afterwards, TR on a track and head through **Gap Farm**. Then continue E on a path. The path runs along the line of HW and you can make out the shape of the Vallum in places. Eventually, arrive at a road: TL for **Hadrian's Holiday Lodges B&B** (0.4 miles) or TR to continue on Stage 4c. Pass a surviving piece of HW emerging from the road embankment. A few minutes later, TL. Shortly afterwards, cross railway tracks when the light is green: look both ways.

8 0:40: Just afterwards, reach a junction: TR for the **Greenhead Detour** (see box) or keep SH to continue on Stage 4c. A few minutes later, at **Thirlwall Castle** (see box), TR on a track.

S 0:45: Cross a footbridge and immediately afterwards, arrive at **Holmhead Guest House**.

 Willowford Bridge Abutment

The E abutment is all that is visible of the Romans' bridge over the River Irthing. It is now on dry land because the course of the Irthing has moved W over time. There were a number of bridges built at this site but the earliest one was probably built under Hadrian at the same time as HW. On the N side of the abutment, there are two sluices with an open channel beside them: the channel was possibly a mill race with the sluices helping to control the flow of water through it.

 Harrow's Scar Milecastle (49)

Little remains of this milecastle but there are still some points of interest. In the 17th century, a cottage was built inside the ruins and you can still see its foundations in the SW corner. The stone milecastle was built on top of the older turf wall milecastle: from here the turf wall and the stone wall followed different courses for two Roman miles W to Milecastle 51.

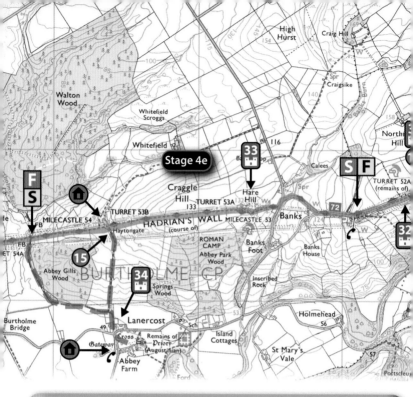

 ## 29 Turret 49b

W of the River Irthing, HW was originally built as a turf wall. Later it was replaced by a stone wall which followed a different course for two Roman miles between Milecastles 49 and 51. Turret 49b was built on the line of, and around the same time as, the stone wall and was bonded fully with it.

 ## 30 Piper Sike Turret (51a)

Unlike Turret 49b, this turret was not bonded fully with HW. It was originally constructed for the turf wall. When the turf wall was replaced by the stone wall, the turret then had to be integrated into it.

 ## 31 Pike Hill Signal Tower

Unfortunately, there is little left of the only known signal tower on HW. It overlooked the Stanegate, a key Roman road which ran E-W from Corbridge to Carlisle. Soldiers would have been able to signal to the nearby forts at Nether Denton and Castle Hill. The tower was built under Trajan, long before HW. The Wall was built with a deliberate kink to incorporate the tower.

 ## 32 Banks East Turret (52a)

Unlike Turret 49b, this turret was not bonded fully with HW. It was originally constructed for the turf wall. When the turf wall was replaced by the stone wall, the turret then had to be integrated into it.

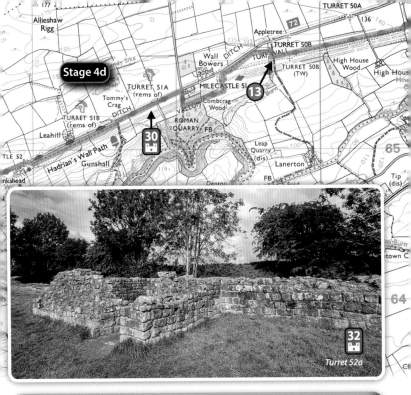

Turret 52a

Hare Hill

This 3m high piece of HW is often claimed to be the highest surviving piece of the structure. However, although the central core is original, the N side of it was actually rebuilt in the 19th century using Roman stones. There is a centurial stone built into the N side: it sits at about head height but is very difficult to spot. The stone was taken from a different part of HW. Most of HW in this area was demolished to build Lanercost Priory in the 12th and 13th centuries. It is therefore a miracle that this fragment survived at all.

Lanercost Priory

The priory was founded somewhere between 1165 and 1174 by Robert de Vaux. It was completed in 1220 and housed priests of the Augustinian religious order. The priory's buildings were built of dressed sandstone, partly using stones from HW: some of the stones have Roman inscriptions. Edward I visited the priory on three occasions: his final visit was in 1306/07 and he died soon afterwards in Burgh-by-Sands.

The priory was dissolved in 1537 by Henry VIII and was granted to Sir Thomas Dacre: the roofs were removed from many buildings but the church continued in use as a parish church. Around 1740, the nave was re-roofed. Much restoration work was carried out on the church in the 19th century. In 1929, the priory was brought into public ownership and is now managed by English Heritage. Visitors can walk around the grounds free of charge but there is a fee to enter the buildings (unless you are an English Heritage member).

131

E-W

Stage 4d: Gilsland to Banks

S From the junction beside the tunnel at the end of Stage 4c, head SW on a path. A few minutes later, pass **Poltross Burn Milecastle (48)**: see page 128. Shortly afterwards, TR and cross train tracks: take great care. Now descend and cross a field: as you descend, notice HW down on the right. A few minutes later, TR and cross a stream on some sleepers. Shortly afterwards, cross a road, bearing right. Then TL onto a path alongside HW again: this is an excellent example of Narrow Wall on broad foundations. Soon pass **Turret 48a**.

10 0:20: Shortly after **Turret 48b**, pass **Willowford Farm B&B**. On one of its buildings, just beside the HWP, there is a centurial stone: this is a stone inscribed by soldiers and built into HW to record which group built the relevant section of curtain. Continue W and a few minutes later, pass **Willowford Bridge Abutment** (see page 129). Shortly afterwards, cross the **River Irthing** on a footbridge: the Irthing was where the turf wall and the stone wall met. Soon climb steps. Then TR at a junction, climbing steeply on a broad path.

11 0:35: TL through the ruins of **Harrow's Scar Milecastle (49)**: see page 129. Afterwards, head W alongside the largest surviving section of the Wall W of the Irthing. There are supposedly some centurial stones still in place on the S side of this part of the Wall, including a phallus. However, at the time of writing, we were unable to locate them: perhaps they are now too weathered to be easily spotted. All of the stone wall on this side of the Irthing was Narrow Wall on narrow foundations.

12 0:50: Arrive at the entrance to **Birdoswald Roman Fort**: head N on the road to head to **Slack House Farm**. To continue on Stage 4d, head briefly W on the road. Just afterwards, TL on a path alongside HW. 5min later, pass **Turret 49b** (see page 130). A few minutes later, the path bends left and climbs to a stone stile: TR and cross it. The HWP now follows the line of the turf wall: you can often see the Ditch and the Vallum with the line of the turf wall between them.

13 1:20: TR on a track. Shortly afterwards, TL, cross a footbridge and continue on a path. 15min later, TL onto a minor road. A few minutes later, pass **Piper Sike Turret (51a)**: see page 130. Soon, TL on a footpath. After a while, pass briefly back onto the road and then re-join the path again, still alongside the road.

Piper Sike Turret

14 2:00: Pass **Pike Hill Signal Tower** (see page 130). A few minutes later, pass **Banks East Turret (52a)**: see page 130. TL onto the road again and descend.

F 2:15: Arrive in **Banks**.

Stage 4e: Banks to Lanercost exit

S From Banks, continue W down the road. Shortly afterwards, TR at a road junction. TL at the next road junction. Shortly afterwards, TR on a track and climb. Shortly after that, reach the section of HW at **Hare Hill** (see page 131).

15 0:25: Arrive at the E exit to **Lanercost Priory** (see page 131). TL for the priory (½ mile), TR for **Haytongate Farm/Barn** or keep SH to continue on Stage 4e. There are picnic tables here and a toilet (just S from the HWP).

F 0:30: Arrive at the W exit to **Lanercost Priory**. TL for the priory (0.7 miles) or keep SH to start Stage 5a.

W-E

Stage 4e: Lanercost exit to Banks

Lanercost Priory

F Continue E.

15 0:05: Arrive at the E exit to Lanercost Priory (see page 131). TR for the priory (½ mile), TL for **Haytongate Farm/Barn** or keep SH to continue on Stage 4e. There are picnic tables here and a toilet (just S of the HWP). After a while, reach the section of HW at **Hare Hill** (see page 131). Shortly afterwards, TL on a road. Shortly after that, TR on another road.

S 0:30: At the next road junction, TL and enter **Banks**.

Stage 4d: Banks to Gilsland

F From Banks, head NE up a road. Soon pick up a path on the right. Pass **Banks East Turret (52a)**: see page 130.

14 0:10: Shortly afterwards, pass **Pike Hill Signal Tower** (see page 130). Continue NE on a path, alongside the road. Pass briefly onto the road again and then re-join the path. After a while, walk along the road yet again. Soon pass **Piper Sike Turret (51a)**: see page 130. Shortly afterwards, TR on a path. 15min later, cross a footbridge and TR on a track.

13 0:55: TL on a path. The HWP now follows the line of the turf wall: you can often see the Ditch and the Vallum with the line of the turf wall between them. After a while, cross a stile and TL. Shortly afterwards, the path bends right. A few minutes later, pass **Turret 49b** (see page 130). 5min later TR onto a road.

12 1:25: Arrive at the entrance to **Birdoswald Roman Fort**: head N on the road to head to **Slack House Farm**. To continue on Stage 4d, pick up a path heading E to the right of a fantastic section of HW. This is the largest surviving section of the Wall W of the Irthing. There are supposedly some centurial stones still in place on the S side of this part of the Wall, including a phallus. However, at the time of writing, we were unable to locate them: perhaps they are now too weathered to be easily spotted. All of the stone wall on this side of the Irthing was Narrow Wall on narrow foundations.

11 1:40: TR through the ruins of **Harrow's Scar Milecastle (49)**: see page 129. Descend steeply on a broad path. TL at a junction. Soon descend steps and cross the **River Irthing** on a footbridge: the Irthing was where the turf wall and the stone wall met. A few minutes later, pass **Willowford Bridge Abutment** (see page 129). Continue E alongside HW.

10 1:55: Arrive at **Willowford Farm B&B**. On one of its buildings, just beside the HWP, there is a centurial stone: this is a stone inscribed by soldiers and built into HW to record which group constructed the relevant section of curtain. Shortly afterwards, pass **Turret 48b**. Continue SE alongside HW: this is an excellent example of Narrow Wall on broad foundations. Soon pass **Turret 48a**. Bear right across a road and pick up a path on the other side. Shortly afterwards, cross a stream on some sleepers and then TL. Cross a field and then climb: notice HW down on the left. Take care crossing train tracks and then TL. Shortly afterwards, pass **Poltross Burn Milecastle (48)**: see page 128.

S 2:15: A few minutes later, reach a junction beside a tunnel: to start Stage 4c, keep SH. To head to Gilsland, TL and go through the tunnel. A few minutes later, arrive at the main street of **Gilsland**.

West of Banks, there are only a few surviving pieces of HW so it is the beautiful English countryside that dominates the attention. This is no bad thing, however, as the scenery is lovely: rolling farmland of the deepest green and paths lined with majestic native trees. Although you rarely see HW, you will frequently follow the line of it: look out for the Ditch and Vallum which appear from time to time as undulations in fields.

Although it is a short distance off the HWP, Lanercost Priory (see page 131) ranks as a highlight of this section and it has relevance to HW too: it was built partly from stones robbed from the Wall. The buildings are open to visitors and the grounds of the priory, which run down to the River Irthing, are wonderful. It is a fabulous experience to combine a priory visit with an overnight stay at Abbey Farm (which is within the walls of the priory).

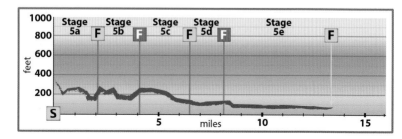

Beautiful deciduous trees on Stage 5a

For some, Carlisle is a shock to the system after many days of country life but for others, it provides an appealing taste of civilisation for the first time since Newcastle. There are plenty of accommodation options in Carlisle, some closer to the HWP than others. If you make the effort to walk all the way into the city centre, you will be rewarded with excellent pubs, restaurants and cafés: it can be quite lively on a Friday or Saturday night!

The Stage is well marked and navigation is straightforward. The terrain is mostly level so there are no big climbs. The paths can be muddy after rain.

		Time	Distance	Ascent	Descent
Stage 5a	Lanercost exit/ Walton	1:00	2.1miles 3.4km	230ft 70m	295ft 90m
Stage 5b	Walton/Newtown	0:45	2.0miles 3.2km	125ft 38m	148ft 45m
Stage 5c	Newtown/Bleatarn Farm	1:00	2.4miles 3.9km	0ft 0m	164ft 50m
Stage 5d	Bleatarn Farm/ Crosby Camping	0:45	1.7miles 2.7km	0ft 0m	0ft 0m
Stage 5e	Crosby Camping/ Carlisle (Sands Centre)	2:00	5.1miles 8.2km	0ft 0m	0ft 0m

Supplies:

Brampton (2.5 miles off Stage 5b/5c) – supermarket & shops

Carlisle (Stage 5e/6a) – supermarkets & shops

Refreshments/Food:

Lanercost Tea Room (½ mile off Stage 4e/5a)

Walton (Stage 5a/5b) – the Reading Room Café & Old Vicarage Bar

Newtown (Stage 5c) – unmanned refreshments stall

Brampton (2.5 miles off Stage 5b/5c)

Crosby Camping (Stage 5d/5e) – drinks

Low Crosby (Stage 5e) – The Stag Inn (closed at the time of writing)

Park Broom Lodge (0.3 miles off Stage 5e)

Carlisle (Stage 5e/6a)

Lanercost Priory

Accommodation:

Lanercost Priory (½ mile off Stage 4e/5a)

Walton (Stage 5a/5b)

Sandysike Bunkhouse & Camping (Stage 5b)

Headswood on the Wall (Stage 5b)

Newtown (Stage 5b/5c)

Brampton (2.5 miles off Stage 5b/5c)

Stonewalls Campsite (1 mile off Stage 5c)

Bleatarn Farm Campsite (Stage 5c/5d)

Crosby Camping (Stage 5d/5e)

Park Broom Lodge (0.3 miles off Stage 5e)

Carlisle (Stage 5e/6a)

Escape/Access:

Lanercost Priory (off-route from Stage 5a/4e)

Newtown (Stage 5b/5c)

Brampton (2.5 miles off Stage 5b/5c)

Oldwall (Stage 5c - Waypoint No.5)

Low Crosby (Stage 5e)

Carlisle (Stage 5e/6a)

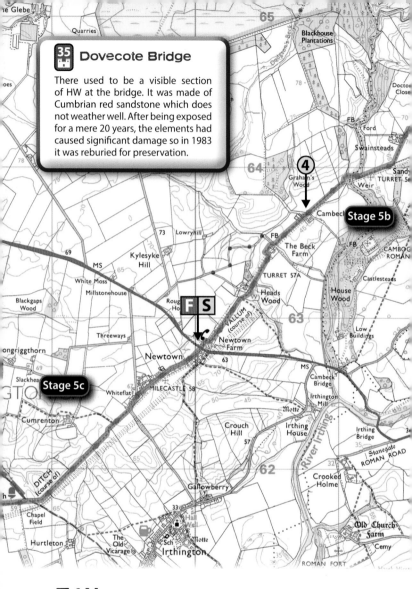

E-W

Stage 5a: Lanercost exit to Walton

S Continue W and shortly afterwards, there are some sections of HW in the trees on the right. 5-10mins later, TR onto a road. Shortly afterwards, TL on a path. When you come to a fence, TL. Shortly afterwards, TR through a gate.

(1) 0:30: TL along a road: the signs state that this is a 'temporary' route but the diversion has been in place for so long now that it seems to be permanent.

(2) 0:50: Just after crossing **Dovecote Bridge**, there is an information board on the right (see box).

F 1:00: Arrive at **Walton**.

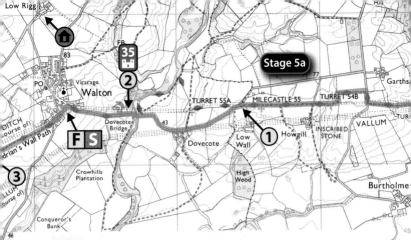

E-W

Stage 5b: Walton to Newtown

S From Walton continue SW along the road. Shortly afterwards, TR on a track. Just afterwards, keep SH onto a grassy path, heading into a field.

③ 0:05: TR at a junction: alternatively, keep SH to reach **Sandysike Bunkhouse**. A few minutes later, TR on a track. A few minutes after that, TL on a farm track. Shortly afterwards, keep SH on a path.

④ 0:25: Keep SH through a farm yard. 5-10mins later, pass **Headswood on the Wall** (Cottage and Glamping Pods).

F 0:45: Arrive at **Newtown**: arrange a taxi from here if you are staying in **Brampton** (2.5 miles SE along the A6071).

W-E

Stage 5b: Newtown to Walton

F From the crossroads at **Newtown**, head NE on a lane and then a path. 10-15min later, pass **Headswood on the Wall** (Cottage and Glamping Pods).

④ 0:20: 5-10min later, keep SH through a farmyard. 15min later, TR on a track. After a few minutes, TL on a path.

③ 0:40: A few minutes later, TL at a junction onto a grassy path, heading through a field: alternatively, TR to reach **Sandysike Bunkhouse**. A few minutes later, keep SH onto a track. Shortly afterwards, TL and head NE along a road.

S 0:45: Arrive at **Walton**.

Stage 5a: Walton to Lanercost exit

F From Walton continue E along the road.

② 0:10: Just before crossing **Dovecote Bridge**, there is an information board on the left (see box). Continue E on the road.

① 0:30: TR on a path. 15min later, go through a gate and then TL alongside a fence. Shortly afterwards, TR (away from the fence) on a faint path: easy to miss. TR onto a road. Shortly afterwards, TL on a path. Soon there are some sections of HW in the trees on the left.

S 1:00: Arrive at the W exit to **Lanercost Priory** (see page 131). TR for the priory (0.7 miles) or keep SH to start Stage 4e.

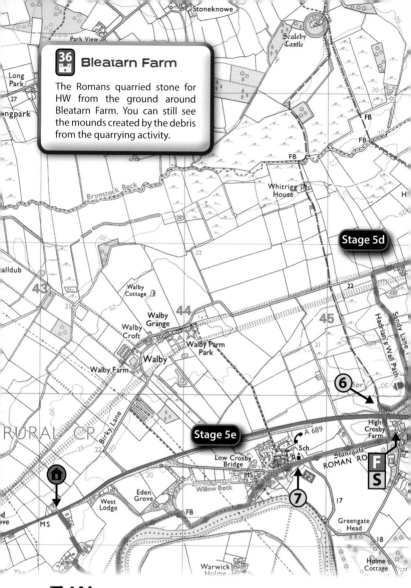

36 Bleatarn Farm

The Romans quarried stone for HW from the ground around Bleatarn Farm. You can still see the mounds created by the debris from the quarrying activity.

E-W

Stage 5c: Newtown to Bleatarn Farm

S From the crossroads at Newtown, head SW on Via Verdi. 5min later, pass the unmanned **Snack Shed**. 5min after that, keep SH at a junction. Shortly afterwards, when the road bends left, TR onto a path. 15min later, just after the path bends right, there is another path on the right: only take this path if you are staying at **Stonewalls Campsite** in Laversdale.

5 0:40: Cross the road at **Oldwall**. Then keep SH on a path.

F 1:00: Arrive at **Bleatarn Farm Campsite** (see box).

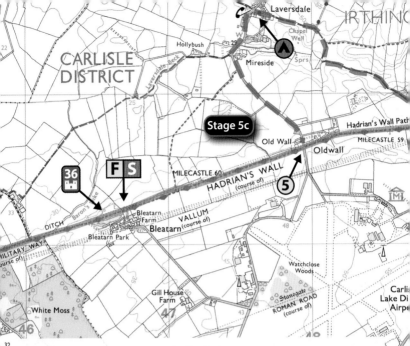

E-W

Stage 5d: Bleatarn Farm to Crosby Camping

S Continue SW on a path through a field. 15min later, keep SH on a lane. After 5min, TL onto another lane.

6 0:40: TL onto a lane. Shortly afterwards, cross a bridge over the A689.

F 0:45: Arrive at **Crosby Camping**.

W-E

Stage 5d: Crosby Camping to Bleatarn Farm

F Head N from Crosby Camping. Shortly afterwards, cross a bridge over the A689.

6 0:05: Shortly after that, TR on a lane. 15min later, TR on another lane. 5min later, keep SH on a path through a field.

S 0:45: Arrive at **Bleatarn Farm Campsite** (see box).

Stage 5c: Bleatarn Farm to Newtown

F From Bleatarn Farm, continue NE on a path.

5 0:20: Cross the road at **Oldwall**: alternatively, TL along the road if you are staying at **Stonewalls Campsite** in Laversdale. Then keep SH on a lane which soon becomes a path. 30min later, keep SH, heading NE on Via Verdi. 5min later, pass the unmanned **Snack Shed**.

S 1:00: 5min later, reach the crossroads at **Newtown**: arrange a taxi from here if you are staying in **Brampton** (2.5 miles SE along the A6071).

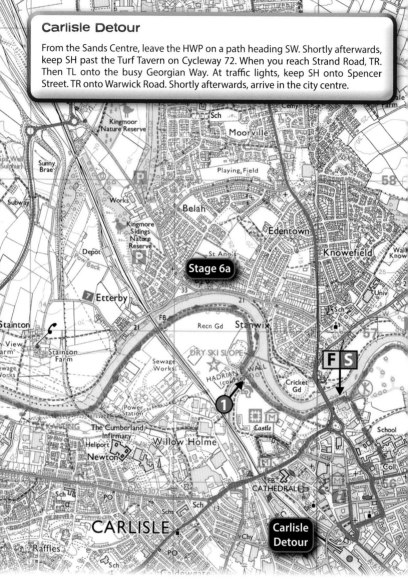

Carlisle Detour

From the Sands Centre, leave the HWP on a path heading SW. Shortly afterwards, keep SH past the Turf Tavern on Cycleway 72. When you reach Strand Road, TR. Then TL onto the busy Georgian Way. At traffic lights, keep SH onto Spencer Street. TR onto Warwick Road. Shortly afterwards, arrive in the city centre.

E-W

Stage 5e: Crosby Camping to Carlisle

S Head S from Crosby Camping. Just afterwards, TR onto a footpath beside a road.

7 0:10: Pass through **Low Crosby**. TL onto Green Lane: at the end of it, keep SH on a path. 20-25min later, TL at a junction: alternatively, keep SH for **Park Broom Lodge.**

8 0:50: Keep SH on a road, ignoring roads to the left and right. A few minutes later, TR at a junction. Immediately afterwards, cross another road. Then TL onto a footpath. Shortly afterwards, cross a bridge over the M6 motorway. Take care on the road when the footpath ends.

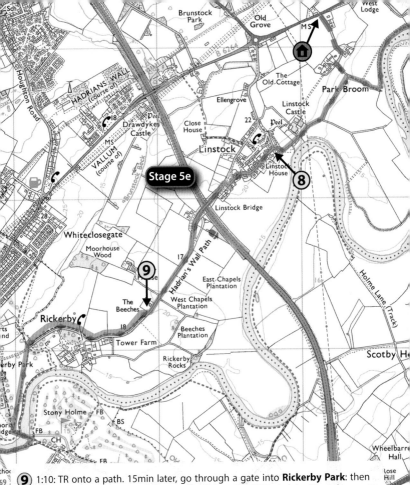

9 1:10: TR onto a path. 15min later, go through a gate into **Rickerby Park**: then bear left on a path through the middle of the park. 5-10min later, TL and cross a steel bridge over the **River Eden**. Immediately afterwards, TR on a path.

F 2:00: Arrive at the **Sands Centre** in **Carlisle**: TL for the **Carlisle Detour** (see box). Otherwise, keep SH to start Stage 6a.

W-E

Stage 5e: Carlisle to Crosby Camping

F From the N side of the Sands Centre, head NE on a path alongside the **River Eden**. 30min later, TL and cross a steel bridge. Afterwards, TR and head NNE through **Rickerby Park**. At the NE side of the park, TR onto a path.

9 0:50: TL onto a road: take care as there is no footpath for a while. Cross a bridge over the M6 motorway. Shortly afterwards, TR onto a road. Immediately afterwards, TL and head NE on another road, ignoring roads to the left and right.

8 1:10: Keep SH on a path. 15-20min later, TR at a junction: alternatively, TL for **Park Broom Lodge**. Keep SH on Green Lane.

7 1:45: Shortly afterwards, TR on a road to head through **Low Crosby**: continue NE on the road out of the village.

S 2:00: TL on a path. Just afterwards, arrive at **Crosby Camping**.

6 Carlisle/ Bowness-on-Solway

You are never far from the water on this section of the HWP. To the W, the route follows paths and minor roads along a flat and starkly beautiful part of the Solway coast. However, to the E a path meanders around the many twists and turns of the River Eden which passes through Carlisle. In-between, there is wonderful rolling countryside to enjoy. There are lovely villages scattered along the route too and most of them have a pub: if you are walking E-W and this will be your last day on the HWP, then you might want to take your time, enjoying a pint along the way.

The Stage is well marked and navigation is straightforward. The terrain is mostly level so there are no big climbs. The paths can be muddy after rain.

On Stages 6b, 6c and 6e, the HWP is at sea level and is prone to tidal flooding during high spring tides. Occasionally, the route is temporarily impassable and you might have to wait until the water level drops. Local accommodation can provide tide tables and there are noticeboards at Dykesfield (W of Burgh-by-Sands) and the E entrance to Bowness-on-

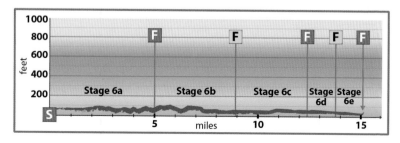

Elevation profile: feet (vertical axis, 200–1000), miles (horizontal axis, 5, 10, 15). Markers: S (start), F (finish points). Stages labelled: Stage 6a, Stage 6b, Stage 6c, Stage 6d, Stage 6e.

The Solway coast on Stage 6e

Solway: the boards show the current month's tidal predictions. Tide information is also available online at www.nationaltrail.co.uk: in the HWP section, go to 'Top Tips for enjoying the Trail'. Alternatively, look at the tide tables for 'Silloth' at www.bbc.co.uk.

Due to the irregularity of public transport from Bowness-on-Solway, many E-W walkers actually get a taxi from Carlisle to Bowness and then walk Section 6 in an easterly direction, back to Carlisle. This means that they finish their final day's walk in Carlisle, enabling a speedy departure by bus or train.

		Time	Distance	Ascent	Descent
Stage 6a	Carlisle (Sands Centre)/Beaumont	2:00	5.0miles 8.1km	262ft 80m	230ft 70m
Stage 6b	Beaumont/Boustead Hill	1:30	3.9miles 6.3km	82ft 25m	180ft 55m
Stage 6c	Boustead Hill/ Glasson	1:30	3.5miles 5.7km	33ft 10m	33ft 10m
Stage 6d	Glasson/Port Carlisle	0:30	1.3miles 2.1km	0ft 0m	0ft 0m
Stage 6e	Port Carlisle/ Bowness-on-Solway	0:30	1.3miles 2.1km	33ft 10m	0ft 0m

Supplies:

Carlisle (Stage 5e/6a)

Grinsdale (Stage 6a) - honesty box selling cold drinks

Burgh-by-Sands (Stage 6b) - water point at St. Michael's Church

Drumburgh (Stage 6c) - Laal Bite at Grange Farm (unmanned snack shop with toilet)

Refreshments/Food:

Carlisle (Stage 5e/6a)

Beaumont (Stage 6a/6b) - Drovers' Rest (off-route)

Burgh-by-Sands (Stage 6b) - Greyhound Inn

Glasson (Stage 6c/6d) - Highland Laddie Inn (closed at the time of writing)

Port Carlisle (Stage 6d/6e) - Hope & Anchor pub

Bowness-on-Solway (Stage 6e)

Coastal flats at Boustead Hill (Stage 6b/6c)

Accommodation

Carlisle (Stage 5e/6a)

Beaumont (Stage 6a/6b)

Boustead Hill (Stage 6b/6c)

Midtown Farm B&B (0.3 miles off Stage 6c)

Glasson (Stage 6c/6d) - Highland Laddie Inn (closed at the time of writing)

Port Carlisle (Stage 6d/6e)

Bowness-on-Solway (Stage 6e)

Escape/Access:

Carlisle (Stage 5e/6a)

Drovers Rest near Beaumont (Stage 6a/6b)

Burgh-by-Sands (Stage 6b)

Glasson (Stage 6c/6d)

Port Carlisle (Stage 6d/6e)

Bowness-on-Solway (Stage 6e)

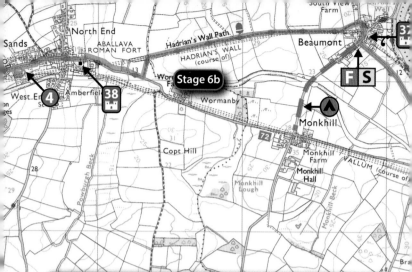

Stage 6b

37 St Mary's Church, Beaumont

The 12th century church was built on the site of Turret 70a. It was constructed from sandstone, partly using stones from HW. In fact, little remains of the original structure: the church was restored on a number of occasions, most recently in the late 19th century. The roof dates from the 16th century.

38 St. Michael's Church, Burgh-by-Sands

The present church dates from the late 12th century. It was built on the site of Aballava Roman Fort, on the line of HW: stones from the Wall were used in its construction. King Edward I died in Burgh-by-Sands and was laid in state in the church before transportation to London.

E-W

Stage 6a: Carlisle to Beaumont

S From the N side of the Sands Centre, head SW on a path alongside the **River Eden**. Shortly after entering **Bitts Park**, keep SH at a broad junction.

1 0:10: 5min later, keep SH at another junction and cross a bridge. Immediately afterwards, TR and continue alongside the river. 1hr later, the path bends left, away from the river. Shortly afterwards, TR on a road into **Grinsdale**. Just afterwards, there is an honesty box selling cold drinks. Shortly afterwards, TL on a path.

2 1:15: Shortly, go through a gate and then head NW on a path. After a while, TR, pass through two gates and then go down steps. Immediately afterwards, TL on a path. Soon, go through a gate and then TL on a path: the original HWP ran directly from here to Beaumont alongside the River Eden, however, landslides have closed that path. At **Kirkandrews-on-Eden**, TR on a road, climbing.

3 1:40: Shortly afterwards, TR on another road, following the route of Hadrian's Cycleway.

F 2:00: Arrive at a junction in **Beaumont**, near **St Mary's Church** (see box): TL for **Roman Wall Lodges** (5min) and the **Drovers' Rest pub** at Monkhill (10min). Alternatively, TR to start Stage 6b.

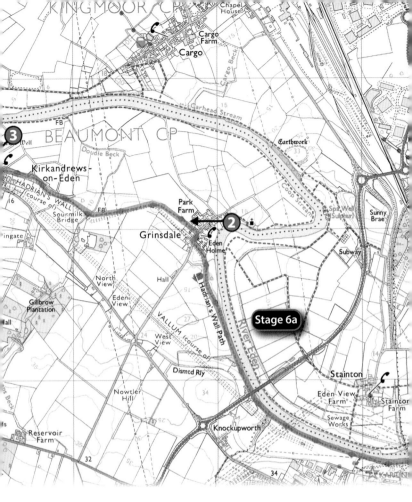

W-E

Stage 6a: Beaumont to Carlisle

F From Beaumont, the original HWP ran beside the River Eden to Kirkandrews-on-Eden, however, landslides have closed that path: instead, from the junction SW of St Mary's Church, head SE on a road, following the route of Hadrian's Cycleway.

3 0:15: TL on another road, descending. A few minutes later, TL on a path. Shortly afterwards, TR, go through a gate and continue on a path. Soon, TR up some steps and go through two gates. Then TL on a path along the side of a field.

2 0:45:TR at a farm yard at **Grinsdale**. Just afterwards, TL through a gate. Shortly after that, TR onto a road. A few minutes later, TL on a path: just before the turning, there is an honesty box selling cold drinks. Soon go through a gate. Then TR at a faint fork and climb gently on a grassy path.

1 1:50: Just after a parking area, TL across a bridge. Shortly afterwards, keep SH into **Bitts Park**. 5min later, TL at a broad junction.

S 2:00: Arrive at the **Sands Centre** in **Carlisle**: TR for the **Carlisle Detour** (see page 142). Otherwise, keep SH to start Stage 5e.

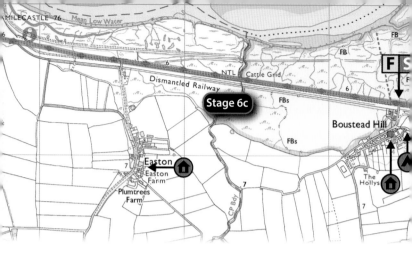

E-W

Stage 6b: Beaumont to Boustead Hill

S From the junction in Beaumont, head NE on the road past **St Mary's Church**. Shortly afterwards, TL in the centre of the village and descend on a road. Shortly after that, TL on a path. Eventually, TR on a road. Shortly afterwards, TR into a field: the path runs parallel to the road. When the path emerges onto the road again, continue W. Shortly afterwards, pass **St. Michael's Church** (see page 148): there is a water point at the back of it. Head W along a village green.

4 0:45: Arrive at the **Greyhound Inn** in the village of **Burgh-by-Sands** (pronounced 'Bruff-by-Sands'): beside it there is a statue of King Edward I (see image below), who died nearby in 1307. Continue W on the road.

F 1:30: Arrive at the signpost at **Boustead Hill**.

Stage 6c: Boustead Hill to Glasson

S From the signpost at Boustead Hill, continue W on the road.

5 0:45: At the village of **Drumburgh** (pronounced 'Drumbruff'), TL onto a lane: alternatively, TR onto another lane for **Laal Bite snack shop**. 15min later, TR. 15min after that, bear left across a field towards a gate: go through it and continue NW on a path through another field. Soon, TR on a road.

F 1:30: 5min later, arrive at the **Highland Laddie Inn** in **Glasson**.

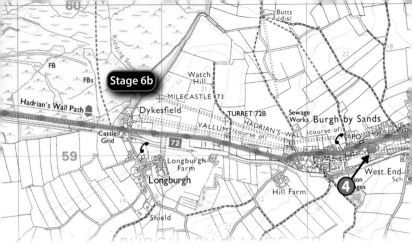

W-E

Stage 6c: Glasson to Boustead Hill

F From the Highland Laddie Inn, head SW on the road through **Glasson**. 5min later, TL onto a path through a field. A few minutes later, go through a gate: then bear left towards another gate in the corner of another field.

5 0:45: At the village of **Drumburgh** (pronounced 'Drumbruff'), TR onto a road: alternatively, keep SH onto a lane for **Laal Bite snack shop**.

S 1:30: Arrive at the signpost at **Boustead Hill**.

Stage 6b: Boustead Hill to Beaumont

F From the signpost at Boustead Hill, continue E on the road.

4 0:45: Reach the **Greyhound Inn** in the village of **Burgh-by-Sands** (pronounced 'Bruff-by-Sands'). Just afterwards, pass the statue of King Edward I who died nearby in 1307: head E along the village green. Shortly afterwards, continue E along the road. Pass **St. Michael's Church** (see page 148): there is a water point at the back of it. Shortly afterwards, TL into a field: the path runs parallel to the road. Shortly, the path emerges onto the road again: continue E. Shortly afterwards, TL onto a path.

S 1:30: TR at a junction and climb on a road into the village of **Beaumont**. Head SW on the road past **St Mary's Church** (see page 148). At a junction, keep SH for **Roman Wall Lodges** (5min) and the **Drovers' Rest pub** at **Monkhill** (10min). Alternatively, TL to start Stage 6a.

The beautiful countryside on Stage 6a

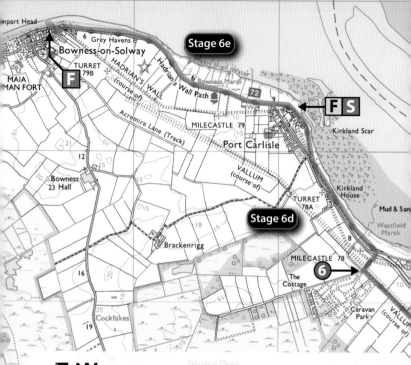

E-W

Stage 6d: Glasson to Port Carlisle

S From the Highland Laddie Inn, head NW.

6 0:15: TR in front of **Glendale Holiday Park**. A few minutes later, cross a road and pick up a path heading NW along the coast.

F 0:30: Reach a bend in the road on the N side of **Port Carlisle**: TL on the road to enter the village. Alternatively, keep SH to start Stage 6e.

Stage 6e: Port Carlisle to Bowness-on-Solway

S From the bend in the road on the N side of Port Carlisle, head W along the coast.

F 0:30: In **Bowness-on-Solway**, TR on a path heading N between buildings. Shortly afterwards, arrive at a wooden shelter facing the sea. Congratulations! You have completed the HWP.

W-E

To reach the start of the HWP, from the E side of Bowness-on-Solway, take a path heading N between buildings. Shortly afterwards, arrive at a wooden shelter facing the sea: this is the start point.

Stage 6e: Bowness-on-Solway to Port Carlisle

F From the shelter, retrace your steps back to Bowness-on-Solway. TL along the road.

S 0:30: The road bends sharply right at the entrance to **Port Carlisle**: stay on the road to enter the village. Alternatively, TL onto a path to start Stage 6d.

W-E

Stage 6d: Port Carlisle to Glasson

From the bend in the road on the N side of Port Carlisle, take a path heading along the coast. Cross a road and walk up a lane.

6 0:15: A few minutes later, TL in front of **Glendale Holiday Park**.

S 0:30: Arrive at the **Highland Laddie Inn** in **Glasson**.

KNIFE EDGE
Outdoor Guidebooks

We thought guidebooks were boring so we decided to change them. Mapping is better than 40 years ago. Graphics are better than 40 years ago. Photography is better than 40 years ago. So why have walking guidebooks remained the same?

Well our guidebooks are **different**:

- ▶ **We use Real Maps.** You know, the **1:25,000/1:50,000** scale maps that walkers actually use to navigate with. Not sketch maps that get you lost. Real maps make more work for us but we think it is worth it. You do not need to carry separate maps and you are less likely to get lost so we save you time!

- ▶ **Numbered Waypoints** on our Real Maps link to the walk descriptions, making routes easier to follow than traditional text-based guidebooks. No more wading through pages of boring words to find out where you are! You want to look at incredible scenery and not have your face stuck in a book all day. Right?

- ▶ **Colour, colour, colour.** Mountains and cliffs are **beautiful** so guidebooks should be too. We were fed up using guidebooks which were ugly and boring. When planning, we want to be **dazzled** with full-size colour pictures of the **magnificence** which awaits us! So our guidebooks fill every inch of the page with beauty: big, **spectacular** photos of mountains, etc. Oh yeah baby!

- ▶ **More practical size.** Long and slim. Long enough to have Real Maps and large pictures but slim enough to fit in a pocket.

Now all that sounds great to us but we want to know if you like what we have done. So hit us with your feedback: good or bad. We are not too proud to change.

Follow us for trekking advice, book updates, discount coupons, articles and other interesting hiking stuff.

 www.knifeedgeoutdoor.com

 info@knifeedgeoutdoor.com

 @knifeedgeoutdoor

 @knifeedgeout

 @knifeedgeoutdoor

Facebook Groups

If you have any questions which are not answered in our books, then you can ask the author in one of our Facebook Groups. Updates to our books can be found in the topic sections of the groups.

The group for this book is 'Hadrian's Wall Path Q&A'. The group's URL is **www.facebook.com/groups/HadriansWall**